15
minute vegan
comfort food
simple & satisfying vegan recipes

Katy Beskow

photography by Dan Jones

quadrille

To Mum and Dad

contents

introduction

The breeze catches my face, a coat nestled around me, the sea air is bracing yet refreshing. In times of trouble, this is where you'll find me. Walking along the East Yorkshire coastline in a pair of wellies (no matter what the weather) in search of escapism, clarity and comfort. I pour a steaming hot beaker of tea from my flask, reassured that this home-brewed elixir will keep me warm. On my knee sits a white paper package, which I unwrap with anticipation and care, every layer revealing the seaside aroma of malt vinegar, rising with the steam of the chips. Some chips have skin on, others don't, but all are sprinkled with salt and vinegar. They're piping hot, crisp on the outside and fluffy on the inside. There's no elegance, nothing fancy, not even a wooden fork, but at that moment, I find comfort.

Comfort food is something that will make you feel better. Whether it is an instant comfort when you're eating it, the mindful process of cooking for family or just yourself, or the nostalgia that takes you back to a happy place. Sometimes it's a meal you've created, or sometimes it's a bag of chips eaten at the beach. Wherever you find comfort food, sit back and enjoy it.

Vegan comfort food can be simple and effortless. You can also take comfort from the fact that your food is cruelty free, ethical and sustainable, with nobody suffering for your moments of pleasure. And those moments are important. Let's get away from the phrase 'guilty pleasure', as you should never feel guilty about the food you're enjoying, just enjoy the choice you've made.

Having hours to spend in the kitchen is a luxury, one that should be enjoyed and fulfilled to create culinary magic! For most, including myself, this luxury is not always possible, but limited time doesn't have to mean limited creativity, and all of these recipes have been tried and tested to be on your plate in fifteen minutes or less. This is a wonderful thing at a time of need, when all you want is to be comforted by a special dish. People often associate comfort foods with a long cooking time – a misconception that also applies to vegan cooking.

Finding comfort in food is personal, from the shopping process to the way you eat it. There's nothing comforting about having to travel to lots of specialist food shops to find weird and wonderful ingredients, so you'll find all the ingredients in this book are readily available at supermarkets.

I've arranged the book into five chapters: Comfort Classics, Social, Solo, Sides & Bites and Sweet. There really is something for everyone at every time, whether you are vegan or not. If you're not a confident cook, you'll find these recipes easy to follow, with familiar flavour combinations.

I hope this book empowers you to create moments of comfort, no matter how little time you have.

what is comfort food?

Sometimes, there's just that one thing that will make you feel better after a day that has not gone according to plan. That mouthful of something humble can evoke memories of happier times, just when you need reminding. Perhaps you just deserve something nourishing, flavourful and homemade, with no good reason other than you fancy it.

Comfort food makes us feel better. It can nourish more than just the body, but the mind and the soul too, which is exactly what food should be about. Comfort food isn't simply about getting nutrition from certain foods for the sake of physical health, but enjoying the cooking and eating experience, with all the satisfying moments that make you feel happy, secure and at home, wherever you are.

Everyone has their favourite comfort foods. And comfort food can be whatever you want it to be, as long as it makes you feel good. Perfectly imperfect, unpretentious and made with love are the common ingredients in all comfort foods – everything else is up to you. Whether you want to eat it from your favourite bowl, from a tub on a picnic blanket or from a paper bag at the seaside, comfort food is all about tasting your food and enjoying the moment.

Comfort food is often associated with autumnal and wintry foods: think casseroles and golden pastries, anything creamy and of course, sugar-coated puddings. These may not be commonly associated with vegan food, and especially vegan food that can be prepared in fifteen minutes. It is a misconception that vegan comfort food takes hours to prepare, as without any meat, fish, eggs or dairy products there are fewer food-safety risks, and the basic ingredients can be easy and quick to cook. Embrace new ingredients (or those unopened ones at the back of your storecupboard). It's also very easy to substitute familiar products with vegan alternatives, which are now widely available and affordable. Vegan cooking is easy when you step out of the 'meat-and-two-veg' way of thinking. There's no limitation to what you can create, with familiar kitchen equipment and no specialist cookery skills required.

Alongside the operational ease of cooking vegan comfort food the fast, easy way, you can rest assured that the food you are eating is cruelty free. When you make the ethical decision to lead a vegan lifestyle, or create a meal that is vegan, you are making a conscious choice to be cruelty free, where no animals are exploited.

Take comfort in the ethical choice you've made, alongside enjoying the delicious food you've created. An increasing number of people are choosing to lead vegan lifestyles for many different reasons, including ethical values, sustainability, reduction of food costs and environmental issues, and more people are questioning where their food comes from and the production methods used. This in turn makes cooking and eating a more mindful process, being aware of what your food is and how it makes you feel. Veganism brings a new dimension to comfort food, where you will find comfort in your choices, as well as in the bowl of food you have in front of you.

choosing your ingredients

Shopping for ingredients is the first step to creating the perfect plate of comfort food, whether you are eating alone or cooking for friends and family. Choose with compassion, be tempted by what looks delicious and never be afraid to try something new. All the ingredients in this book can be found at supermarkets, so you won't have to visit multiple shops before you can start cooking. When buying any processed ingredients, do ensure they are vegan friendly by looking out for labelling or reading the ingredients list. There is a host of resources available online to help understand which ingredients, including E numbers, are from animal sources, but labelling on packaging is improving all the time to make this easier.

plant-based milks, yoghurt, cream and cheese

Dairy-free milk, yoghurt and cream are versatile ingredients that can be used in both savoury and sweet dishes. Many brands are ultra-heat treated (UHT), so they have a long shelf life, making them perfect to keep in your kitchen cupboard or fridge ready to create comfort food when you need it most. There are many brands and varieties of non-dairy milks, including soya, almond, oat, cashew and hemp. Soya and almond milks are the most versatile to use in cooking, but try a few and choose your favourite. Supermarket own brand plant-based milks can be excellent quality and worth a try in your cooking, rather than splashing out on branded products. Vegan yoghurt products tend to be soya or coconut based, making them perfect to use in smooth sauces in savoury dishes, but also

to add to desserts or as a simple breakfast with fruit. Unsweetened soya yoghurts are the most versatile for cooking, but look out for vanilla flavours for instant sweetness to puddings. You'll find soya and oat single cream in the chiller fridges and often UHT on the ambient shelves. These add luxurious texture to sauces and puddings in an instant. Soft and hard vegan cheeses can be found in large supermarkets, usually in their 'free-from' refrigerated sections. Just like dairy cheeses, they add instant flavour and a smooth texture to dishes.

vegan butter

In this book, the term 'vegan butter' refers to vegan margarine or spread that is widely available in supermarkets. Some varieties are 'accidentally vegan' due to the manufacturer using vegetable-based fats rather than dairy, so be sure to read the labelling and ingredients lists. There are many brands on the market and it's worth trying a few to decide which you prefer. Vegan butter is for more than just spreading on toast; use it for baking, enriching sauces and making dairy-free buttercream.

fresh vegetables and fruits

Many people go into auto-pilot mode when buying vegetables and fruit, choosing items they are familiar cooking with. Start really looking at the selection of produce available and focus on what looks fresh and appetising. Use your instincts on what looks interesting and get excited about your choices. If you choose an item you've never cooked with before, enquire if it's in season, as fresh produce that is in season will have more flavour, may have travelled

less and will be cheaper to purchase. When you're creating vegan comfort food in fifteen minutes, consider choosing softer vegetables that can be cooked quickly, such as aubergines, mushrooms, peppers and spinach. Root vegetables that traditionally take longer to cook, such as carrots, sweet potatoes and butternut squash can be incorporated into your dish in fifteen minutes using various preparation and cooking techniques, but if you wish to speed up this process, many root vegetables freeze well and can be found in the supermarket freezer pre-prepared, saving you time. Be aware that while shiny fruit looks tempting, it may have been coated with shellac, an animal ingredient. Fruits most likely to have been treated this way include oranges, lemons and limes, so be sure to choose unwaxed varieties to brighten the flavour of your dishes. Soft fruits, including berries, cherries and peaches have the fastest cooking time and are perfect for a comforting pudding.

pastry

Shop-bought pastry stored in the fridge or freezer makes the perfect base to both savoury and sweet dishes, and I make no apologies for using it, as it is convenient, fast and can create so many comforting meals. Many brands of pastry are accidentally vegan as they use vegetable oil instead of dairy butter, but always read the ingredients before purchasing. If your freezer space allows, keep a selection of shortcrust, puff and filo to hand, and simply bring it to room temperature before using. The ready-rolled varieties are extra time saving.

pasta

Pasta is the main ingredient for so many comfort food dishes, as well as being the ultimate fast food. Most dried pasta varieties will simply contain wheat flour and durum wheat semolina, whereas the fresh varieties are more likely to contain eggs. Dried pasta has the benefit of a long storage life, meaning it will be in your cupboard when you need that big bowl of Spaghetti alla puttanesca (page 78). Store in an airtight container, such as a tall jar and keep a few varieties and shapes in your cupboard.

canned beans and pulses

Cooking beans and pulses from dried form can take hours, including a long soaking time. As beans and pulses are the building blocks of vegan protein as well as being versatile ingredients for so many dishes, I recommend using canned varieties when cooking in fifteen minutes. Stock up on canned chickpeas, butter beans, red kidney beans and green lentils, then simply drain away the salted water they are stored in and rinse thoroughly in cold water to remove any 'canned' taste. Pressure cookers can also be used to cook dried beans and lentils in a shorter amount of time, then you can cool and freeze the beans in batches ready for use in a recipe at a later date. Edamame beans, broad beans and peas are available in the freezer sections of most supermarkets – these varieties keep their flavour and texture well during the freezing process, meaning they can be added to your dish and ready in just moments.

spices and herbs

Add instant flavour to any sweet or savoury dish with the addition of fresh or dried herbs and spices. Build up a selection of versatile spices, including cinnamon, cumin, nutmeg and turmeric, and have a few spice blends available for fast flavouring, including chilli powder and jerk seasoning. Store spices in a dry, dark place to preserve their unique flavours. Woody herbs such as rosemary, thyme and oregano work well from dried, whereas leafy herbs such as coriander, basil and flat-leaf parsley always taste better fresh. Store fresh herbs stalks-down in a glass of water, in a light environment for freshness. Never underestimate the power of a scattering of fresh herbs over a finished dish to add layers of zesty flavour and vibrant colour.

rice

Clouds of seasoned rice make for a perfect side dish or a delicious main dish, such as my Garden biryani (page 46). Basmati rice has the shortest cooking time and has a wonderful flavour, so save the long-grain and wild rices for when you have more time to spend in the kitchen.

alcohol

Adding wine or beer to a dish gives a depth of flavour, but do ensure what you are using is suitable for vegans. Some products contain isinglass, an animal product used to clarify the liquid, or even gelatine and eggs. Some brands clearly label vegan-friendly wines and beers, but if you are unsure, contact the supplier or use an online resource.

salt

Salt enhances the flavour of a dish with minimal effort. I'd recommend using good-quality salt flakes to crumble onto food for a clear flavour and no unnecessary additives often found in the highly processed fine salts.

sugar

A versatile storecupboard essential, sugar can be used to reduce the acidity in tomato-based dishes and of course, to add familiar sweetness to puddings. In the UK, all sugar is vegan friendly as it is not filtered through, or mixed with, animal ingredients, but check before purchasing as manufacturers can change their processes. When consumed moderately, sugar is a magical ingredient found in many comfort foods.

the comfort food kitchen

You don't need an extensive kitchen to create vegan comfort food fast, but a few pieces of equipment can speed up the process and make cooking easier.

pressure cooker

A pressure cooker is a useful piece of equipment to have in your kitchen to create comfort food fast. Not only can pressure cookers revolutionise the way you cook, but they can preserve essential nutrients in food that slow cooking can lose. Pressure cooking appeared to go out of fashion some time ago, as the old-style pan pressure cookers were often perceived as dangerous to have rattling on the stove. However, they are now modernised with simple release functions, and some are electric with multi-use features. Pressure cooking works by creating steam from the liquid in the food, which is then trapped within the cooker. This causes a constant balance between heat and pressure, which cooks your food faster. Because of this, there must always be liquid present in the pan to create the steam. Feeling inspired? Try my Risotto caprese (page 98). Pressure cookers can also be used to bulk cook beans and pulses from dried if you don't wish to use canned. When the beans or pulses are cooked, you can let them cool before freezing them in portions, so they are ready to use at any time.

knives

Never underestimate the value of a few good-quality knives. You don't need a whole chef's collection, but a decent small, medium, large and bread knife will allow you to prepare ingredients with ease and speed. Choose knives with an ergonomic handle and chop on a wooden board to absorb the impact and protect you and your knives. A good-quality T-bar vegetable peeler is also useful.

deep-fat fryer

If you love cooking comfort food at home, a deep-fat fryer is a time-saving piece of equipment. It's perfect for homemade chips, churros, tempura and banana fritters. Like with all fried foods, eat in moderation but enjoy them when you do! If you don't have a deep-fat fryer, you can use a deep pan on the stove. Be sure to only ever fill a deep pan half-way with oil to avoid injury and never leave it unattended. Choose sunflower oil as your frying oil, as it is flavourless, cost effective and has a high smoke point.

blender

Invest in a high-powered blender to create silky-smooth soups and sauces, pesto and homemade houmous on demand! Blenders are also useful for combining and crushing spices. Aim for a model that comes complete with a jug and a power of over 1000W.

microwave

Microwaves are resident in many kitchens, but often, they are just used to reheat food. Liberate your microwave and use it to its full potential for fast comfort food. You can steam fresh vegetables, cook rice, prepare a quick jacket potato and of course, bake super-fast mug cakes.

five steps to comfort food

Buy ingredients that look enticing. Be inspired by colourful, fragrant and seasonal produce, and try new things often. Sometimes, this means stepping outside of the supermarket to a local food market, where you can smell and feel the products, as well as chatting to the vendor about the locality and sourcing of the produce for sale. Choose vegan alternatives for an ethical and sustainable way to eat. Be excited about your purchases and plan how you will use up every last bite to reduce waste.

1) Enjoy being in the kitchen – even if you only have fifteen minutes to spare. Pour yourself a glass of wine or brew a cup of tea and enjoy the mindful process of following a recipe and putting a delicious meal together, whether you are cooking for yourself or friends and family. Be spontaneous and adapt recipes to your own preferences, like adding a little extra chilli if you like more heat or switching one fresh ingredient for another – cooking is all about what is right for you. Cooking is also about having fun and being creative, so don't take yourself too seriously!

2) Plate up your food onto your favourite crockery, whether it's a plate you usually keep for special occasions, an old chipped bowl that reminds you of dinner at your gran's house, or load it into lunch tubs to take on a picnic. Eating from your favourite plate or bowl always feels like home, as it's familiar and comforting. Enjoy your comfort food somewhere you feel happy, whether it's being curled up on the sofa or sat under the tree in the park; there are no rules.

3) Eat together when you can and turn each meal into a catch-up, celebration or conversation. It feels great to cook up a feast for family and friends and have everyone help themselves to a selection of foods. Set up a table with fresh linens, perhaps some flowers and always plenty of serving spoons for guests to try out new dishes. Some of the happiest memories people have are when families get together and sit around the table to enjoy a meal. This isn't exclusively for a special occasion or celebration, but simple, everyday mealtimes spent with immediate family. Eating like this creates memories and a positive, holistic attitude towards food.

4) Sometimes we choose to eat alone, whether it's a conscious choice, irregular work shifts, or just what we need to do to enjoy a moment of 'me time'. When cooking for yourself, you're more likely to try something new, so take the opportunity to choose a recipe you fancy cooking and get creative with the ingredients. Cooking for yourself is rewarding, from the process through to eating, where you can relax and enjoy the food, tasting every mouthful.

5) It's easy to get stuck in a rut when cooking for yourself and for others, creating dishes that you're familiar with, perhaps out of habit. This becomes uninspiring in the kitchen and at the dinner table, so use any opportunity to try something original – who knows, it could become your new comfort food classic! Every familiar dish started with an idea in the kitchen, so get creative, break the rules and eat the type of food you love, just the way you like it.

comfort classics

When all you need is something simple, nourishing
and comforting, choose one of these recipes
to soothe and satisfy.

tuscan bean
and pasta soup

Serves 4

The reassuring texture and flavour of white beans and pasta are brought together in this simple soup, which is filling and warming.

Butterfly-shaped farfalle look attractive, as well as being easy to eat from a spoon.

Heat the olive oil in a large saucepan over a medium–high heat and cook the onion, celery and carrot for 3–4 minutes, stirring frequently. Add the garlic, oregano and mixed herbs, and cook for a further minute.

Pour in the chopped tomatoes, hot vegetable stock, pasta and cannellini beans, and cook for 8 minutes, with the pan lid placed over on an angle. Stir occasionally.

Add the kale and cook for a further 2 minutes.

Season to taste with sea salt and black pepper.

1 tbsp olive oil

1 onion, finely chopped

1 stick of celery, finely chopped

1 carrot, finely chopped

1 clove of garlic, crushed

1 tsp dried oregano

1 tsp dried mixed herbs

400g (14oz) can chopped tomatoes

1 litre (1¾ pints/4½ cups) hot vegetable stock

100g (3½oz) farfalle pasta (ensure egg free)

400g (14oz) can cannellini beans, drained and rinsed

Generous handful of kale, stalks removed

Sea salt and black pepper

comfort classics

caramelised onion, thyme and fig tartlets

Serves 4

There's something about the aroma of caramelising onions that transports me to autumn. Wrapping up warm, walking over crispy leaves and enjoying comfort food as the afternoon becomes evening are what the season is all about. Not only do these golden tartlets look like they belong in the autumn, the sweet, earthy flavours and flaky pastry are comforting when it's cold outside.

—

Preheat the oven to 200°C/400°F/gas mark 6.

Place the pastry quarters onto two baking trays. Use a knife to score around the edges of each pastry quarter to form a border. Using a fork, gently pierce the centre of the pastry a few times. Brush the edges with the soya milk, then bake for 10–12 minutes until golden and puffed.

In the meantime, heat the oil in a frying pan and cook the onions over a medium heat for 5 minutes. Stir in the sugar and thyme, and increase the heat to medium–high. Cook for a further 6–7 minutes until brown and caramelised.

Remove the pastry from the oven and arrange on plates. Spoon the caramelised onions into the centre of the tartlets. Place a slice of fig on top and serve while hot.

1 sheet of ready-rolled puff pastry (ensure dairy free), cut into quarters

1 tsp soya milk, for glazing

2 tbsp olive oil

4 large onions, finely sliced

1 tsp soft brown sugar

½ tsp dried thyme

1 fresh fig, finely sliced from top to bottom

comfort classics

herby white wine mushrooms on toast

Serves 2

Mushrooms sautéed with white wine and herbs are served on toasted sourdough to make the most perfect brunch.

―――――

Ensure that your white wine is vegan by checking the label or using one of the many online resources. Some wines contain animal ingredients used in the clarifying process.

Gently heat the olive oil in a frying pan and add the mushrooms. Increase the heat to medium–high and sauté for 5–6 minutes until the mushrooms begin to soften.

Spoon in the white wine, rosemary and thyme, and cook for a further 5–6 minutes, stirring frequently, until the wine has reduced.

In the meantime, toast the sourdough bread slices until golden, then arrange on plates and drizzle with the extra virgin olive oil.

Remove the mushrooms from the heat and stir through the parsley. Season to taste with sea salt and black pepper. Spoon the mushrooms over the toast and serve while hot.

1 tbsp olive oil

10 chestnut (cremini) mushrooms, roughly sliced

2 tbsp white wine (ensure vegan)

½ tsp dried rosemary

½ tsp dried thyme

4 thick slices of sourdough bread

2 tsp good-quality extra virgin olive oil

Handful of fresh flat-leaf parsley, finely chopped

Generous pinch of sea salt and black pepper

loaded tortilla chips with lime yoghurt

Serves 2

A mountain of hot, crisp tortilla chips, feisty red chillies and cooling lime-infused yoghurt make for the perfect comfort food – they are almost too good to share!

———

Serve as a side to the Chocolate chilli (page 26), or enjoy as a snack.

Preheat the oven to 200°C/400°F/gas mark 6.

Arrange the tortilla triangles on a baking tray and scatter with the chilli flakes. Drizzle with sunflower oil and rub the oil over the triangles to evenly coat. Bake for 8 minutes until golden and crisp, then carefully place the hot chips into a large bowl.

Sprinkle over the red chilli, spring onion, coriander and smoked sea salt, then add the avocado.

Spoon on the soya yoghurt and sprinkle the lime zest over the top.

2 soft tortillas, cut into rough triangles

½ tsp dried chilli flakes

Drizzle of sunflower oil

1 red chilli, deseeded and finely sliced

1 spring onion (scallion), finely sliced

Small handful of fresh coriander (cilantro), roughly chopped

Generous pinch of smoked sea salt

1 small avocado, peeled and finely sliced

2 tbsp unsweetened soya yoghurt

Zest of 1 unwaxed lime

comfort classics

watermelon gazpacho

Serves 4

In the same way that a hot bowl of soup is comforting on a cold day, this cool gazpacho is welcoming and refreshing during the warmer months.

———

Keep the watermelon and cucumber chilled before blending, for an instantly cool gazpacho.

Put the tomatoes, red pepper and onion into a high-powered blender and blitz until semi-smooth.

Add the cucumber and watermelon and blitz until completely smooth.

Serve in bowls, scattered with the avocado and coriander, and add Tabasco sauce to taste.

4 tomatoes, quartered

1 red (bell) pepper, roughly chopped

1 small red onion, roughly chopped

½ chilled cucumber, roughly chopped

½ chilled watermelon, flesh roughly chopped and seeds removed

1 avocado, finely chopped

Small handful of fresh coriander (cilantro), finely chopped

A few drops of Tabasco sauce

comfort classics

storecupboard tomato soup

Serves 4

There's nothing quite like a steamy bowl of tomato soup in cold weather. Many shop-bought varieties contain milk, but this cheat's version uses ingredients from your pantry to create a rich and smooth soup to warm and comfort in no time at all.

Using a high-powered blender will whisk the ingredients into a rich, silken soup.

Heat the olive oil in a large saucepan and sauté the onion over a medium–high heat for 2–3 minutes until it begins to soften. Add the garlic and cook for a further minute.

Pour in the chopped tomatoes and stock, then spoon in the sugar. Allow to bubble for 10 minutes until the onion becomes translucent.

Shake in the Worcestershire sauce, then carefully tip into a high-powered blender. Blitz until creamy and smooth.

Season to taste with salt and black pepper and pour into bowls. Scatter with the basil leaves just before serving.

1 tbsp olive oil

1 onion, finely sliced

1 clove of garlic, crushed

400g (14oz) can good-quality chopped tomatoes

500ml (17½fl oz/2 cups) hot vegetable stock

1 tbsp caster (superfine) sugar

3–4 drops vegan Worcestershire sauce (ensure anchovy free)

Pinch of sea salt and black pepper

Handful of fresh basil leaves, torn

comfort classics

herby pea soup

Serves 4

I love this storecupboard soup, which is creamy and vibrant, as well as being ready to eat in less than 15 minutes.

––––––––––

This soup is delicious as part of a picnic. Ladle into an insulated flask while hot and swirl over the soya cream just before eating.

Heat the olive oil in a large saucepan over a medium heat and cook the onion for 2–3 minutes until softened but not browned. Add the garlic and chilli flakes, and cook for a further minute.

Pour in the frozen peas and vegetable stock and cook for 10 minutes.

Remove from the heat and carefully ladle into a high-powered blender. Blitz until smooth, then stir in the parsley and mint. Season to taste with sea salt and black pepper, then squeeze in the lemon juice.

Pour into bowls and finish with a swirl of soya cream, and a sprinkle of chilli flakes if you like.

1 tbsp olive oil

1 onion, finely chopped

1 clove of garlic, crushed

½ tsp dried chilli flakes, extra for garnish

300g (10oz/2 cups) frozen peas

800ml (scant 1½ pints/ 3½ cups) hot vegetable stock

Generous handful of fresh flat-leaf parsley, finely chopped

Generous handful of fresh mint leaves, finely chopped

Generous pinch of sea salt and black pepper

Juice of ½ unwaxed lemon

4 tbsp soya cream, to finish

chickpea and chard korma

Serves 4 generously

This creamy, comforting korma is perfect served with clouds of basmati rice, or with warmed naan bread. Swiss chard offers a slight bitterness to the sweet and rich coconut milk base.

———

Concentrated korma paste adds all of your favourite spices, with minimal effort. Check the ingredients to ensure the paste is free from dairy.

Heat the sunflower oil in a large frying pan, add the onion and soften over a medium–high heat for 2–3 minutes. Add the garlic and Swiss chard, and sauté for a further minute.

Stir through the cumin and turmeric, then add the korma paste, coating the onion and Swiss chard.

Pour in the coconut milk and chickpeas, then allow to bubble for 10 minutes.

Season to taste with sea salt and scatter with the coriander.

1 tbsp sunflower oil

1 onion, finely chopped

2 cloves of garlic, crushed

4 large leaves of Swiss chard, stalks removed and roughly chopped

1 tsp ground cumin

½ tsp turmeric

1 tbsp korma paste (ensure dairy free)

400ml (14fl oz) can full-fat coconut milk

400g (14oz) can chickpeas, drained and rinsed

Pinch of sea salt

Small handful of fresh coriander (cilantro), roughly torn

chocolate chilli

Serves 4

This is soul food in a bowl. The fiery, fresh, dark and deep flavours marry together to create this indulgent chilli, which tastes like it's been cooking for hours. For those who are sceptical about the addition of cocoa, you'll find this dish has a beautifully balanced richness and a satisfyingly dark sauce.

This chilli freezes perfectly, so whip up a pan, enjoy a portion and pop the rest in the freezer for evenings when you have less than 15 minutes to cook.

Also, be sure your chocolate is dairy free.

Add the chopped tomatoes and onion to a large saucepan over a medium–high heat. Throw in the red pepper, celery and sweetcorn, and cook for 2–3 minutes.

Spoon in the cocoa, chilli powder, sugar, smoked paprika and cinnamon. Stir through the kidney beans and cannellini beans until combined, and cook for 12 minutes, stirring frequently while the chilli bubbles away.

Remove from the heat and scatter with the spring onion, coriander and lime juice. Sprinkle over the dark chocolate just before serving.

400g (14oz) can chopped tomatoes

1 onion, finely sliced

1 red (bell) pepper, deseeded and sliced

1 stick of celery, roughly chopped

4 tbsp frozen or canned sweetcorn

2 tsp each cocoa powder and mild chilli powder

1 tsp each soft brown sugar and smoked paprika

½ tsp ground cinnamon

400g (14oz) can red kidney beans, drained and rinsed and 400g (14oz) can cannellini beans, drained and rinsed

1 spring onion (scallion), roughly chopped

Small handful of fresh coriander (cilantro), roughly torn

Juice of 1 unwaxed lime

1 square of dark chocolate, grated

rainbow pho

Serves 4 generously

Pho is tradionally a Vietnamese soup, fragrant and fresh with slippery noodles. This version is fast and fuss free for comfort food on demand.

Heat the olive oil in a large saucepan and sauté the mushrooms over a medium–high heat for 2 minutes until softened. Add the garlic, cinnamon, ginger, Chinese five spice and soy sauce, and cook for a further minute.

Pour in the hot water and bring to the boil for 5 minutes.

Add the yellow pepper, carrot and spinach, reduce the heat, and simmer for 3 minutes before adding the noodles. Cook for a further 2 minutes until softened.

Ladle into bowls and scatter with the coriander and chilli. Squeeze over the lime juice just before serving.

1 tbsp olive oil

6 button mushrooms, roughly sliced

2 cloves of garlic, finely sliced

1 tsp ground cinnamon

1 tsp ground ginger

½ tsp Chinese five spice

1 tbsp dark soy sauce

1 litre (1¾ pints/4½ cups) hot water

1 yellow (bell) pepper, finely sliced

1 small carrot, grated

Small handful of spinach

300g (10oz) flat rice noodles (ensure egg free)

Generous handful of fresh coriander (cilantro), roughly torn

1 red chilli, finely chopped

Juice of 1 unwaxed lime

comfort classics

red bean goulash

Serves 4

All you'll need with this bowl of goulash is a spoon and a slice of crusty bread to soak up the smoky sauce.

Many supermarkets and health food shops sell vegan soured cream. If you wish, replace the soya yoghurt in this recipe for vegan soured cream for a tangier taste.

Heat the olive oil in a saucepan and sauté the onion, celery and red pepper over a high heat for 2–3 minutes. Add the garlic and cook for a further minute.

Reduce the heat to medium and stir through the smoked and sweet paprika and the rosemary.

Pour in the chopped tomatoes, kidney beans and borlotti beans, then stir through the yeast extract. Place a lid loosely over the pan and allow to simmer for 10 minutes, stirring occasionally.

Remove from the heat and stir through the lemon juice. Serve in bowls, scattered with the parsley, and add a small dollop of soya yoghurt just before serving.

1 tbsp olive oil

1 onion, finely chopped

1 stick of celery, finely chopped

1 red (bell) pepper, finely chopped

1 clove of garlic, crushed

1 rounded tbsp smoked paprika

1 rounded tbsp sweet paprika

½ tsp dried rosemary

400g (14oz) can chopped tomatoes

400g (14oz) can red kidney beans, drained and rinsed

400g (14oz) can borlotti beans, drained and rinsed

1 rounded tsp yeast extract

Juice of ½ unwaxed lemon

Handful of fresh flat-leaf parsley, roughly chopped

2 tbsp unsweetened soya yoghurt

moussaka bowls

Serves 4

I love the sweet, charred flavours of moussaka, but rarely have the time for the oven-baked version to be ready. These bowls contain all the flavours and textures of a slow-cooked moussaka, without the wait.

Start by making the lentil mince. Heat the olive oil in a large saucepan over a medium–high heat and cook the onion for 2–3 minutes until softened but not browned. Add the garlic, cinnamon, paprika and oregano, and cook for 1 minute, stirring constantly.

Pour in the chopped tomatoes, lentils and yeast extract, and simmer for 10 minutes.

In the meantime, prepare the aubergines. Heat a griddle pan until hot.

Brush the aubergine slices with the olive oil and place them on the hot pan, cooking them for 2–3 minutes on each side until softened and grill marks appear. Grill the tomatoes for 1 minute, cut-side down.

Spoon the lentil mince into bowls along with the aubergine slices and griddled tomato halves. Spoon over the soya yoghurt and sprinkle with the grated nutmeg.

Season to taste with sea salt and scatter with the parsley.

comfort classics

For the lentil mince
1 tbsp olive oil

1 onion, finely chopped

1 clove of garlic, crushed

½ tsp ground cinnamon

½ tsp smoked paprika

½ tsp dried oregano

400g (14oz) can chopped
tomatoes

400g (14oz) can green lentils,
drained and rinsed

1 tsp yeast extract

For the aubergines (eggplants)
2 aubergines (eggplants), sliced
into 1cm (½in) rounds

2 tsp olive oil

4 large tomatoes, halved

For the nutmeg yoghurt
and garnish
8 tbsp unsweetened soya yoghurt

Pinch of freshly grated nutmeg

Pinch of flaked sea salt

Handful of fresh flat-leaf
parsley, roughly torn

allotment cobbler

Serves 4

Homemade comfort food at its best.

Preheat the oven to 220°C/425°F/gas mark 7. Line a baking tray with baking paper.

Start by making the scone-dumplings. In a bowl, mix together the flour, rosemary, thyme and salt, then rub in the vegan butter until the mixture resembles breadcrumbs. Stir through the soya milk until a smooth dough is created. Use your hands to flatten the dough to 2.5cm (1in) thick on a lightly floured surface, then use a scone cutter to make eight scone-dumplings. Place them onto the prepared baking tray and brush with a little soya milk. Bake for 10–11 minutes until just golden.

In the meantime, make the filling. In a stove-to-table pot, heat the olive oil over a medium–high heat and cook the leek for 2 minutes. Add the courgette and red pepper, and cook for a further 2 minutes until softened. Throw in the garlic, oregano and mixed herbs, and cook for a further minute.

Pour in the chopped tomatoes, broad beans and ketchup, and cover with the lid. Bubble on high for 7–8 minutes until the vegetables are tender.

Remove the pot from the heat and squeeze over the lemon juice.

Remove the scones from the oven and carefully place them over the cooked filling, pressing them in gently to absorb some sauce. Serve hot.

For the scone-dumplings

160g (5¾oz/1¼ cups) self-raising flour, plus extra for dusting

1 tsp dried rosemary

½ tsp dried thyme

Generous pinch of salt

50g (1¾oz/3½ tbsp) vegan butter

100ml (3½fl oz/scant ½ cup) soya milk, plus 1 tbsp for glazing

For the filling

1 tbsp olive oil

1 leek, finely chopped

1 medium courgette (zucchini), cut into even chunks

1 red (bell) pepper, roughly chopped

2 cloves of garlic, crushed

1 tsp dried oregano

1 tsp dried mixed herbs

400g (14oz) can chopped tomatoes

4 rounded tbsp fresh broad (fava) beans, podded

1 tbsp tomato ketchup

Juice of 1 unwaxed lemon

social

Getting together with a group of friends or family over a meal and bottle of wine is one of life's true pleasures. I love serving up sharing plates, so everyone can get stuck in without any formalities. Serving pots and plates at the table means less preparation in the kitchen and more time to spend with guests. In this chapter, you'll find five menus featuring dishes that work perfectly together and are ideal to share with family or friends.

rustic bistro

Serves 4

1. Chestnut mushroom bourguignon

2. Parsley and butter bean mash

3. Garlic baguettes

4. Fennel and radicchio slaw

5. Mint and mustard green beans

Create a French bistro in your own
home with this rich and comforting meal.

I. chestnut mushroom bourguignon

Delight dinner guests with this deep, boozy, herbed bourguignon.

———

Mushrooms absorb lots of liquid, so cook them in a separate pan to the base sauce to keep them at their best.

In a frying pan, heat 1 tablespoon of the olive oil and cook the mushrooms over a medium–high heat for 10 minutes until softened and fragrant.

In a separate large saucepan, heat the remaining olive oil and sauté the shallots and carrot over a medium–high heat for 4 minutes until the carrot begins to soften. Add the garlic, thyme and rosemary, and sauté for a further minute, then sprinkle in the flour and ensure the vegetables are well coated.

Pour the wine and ketchup into the shallot pan, stir through and allow to reduce for 10 minutes, adding the hot water when the sauce starts to thicken.

Spoon the cooked mushrooms and any juices into the saucepan and season to taste with sea salt and black pepper.

2 tbsp olive oil

600g (1lb 5oz) chestnut (cremini) mushrooms, brushed clean and halved

6 shallots, halved

1 carrot, sliced

1 clove of garlic, crushed

½ tsp dried thyme

½ tsp dried rosemary

3 tsp plain (all-purpose) flour

200ml (7fl oz/generous ¾ cup) red wine (ensure vegan)

1 tbsp tomato ketchup

150ml (5¼fl oz/generous ½ cup) hot water

Pinch of sea salt and black pepper

2. parsley and butter bean mash

Lemony, herby butter beans make the most perfect mash, and best of all, it's ready in under 10 minutes.

———————

Bring the lemon to room temperature before use, so it becomes easier to juice.

Tip the butter beans into a saucepan. Cover with boiling water and simmer for 5 minutes, then drain and rinse in boiling water.

Stir through the parsley, olive oil and lemon juice, then use a potato masher to mash until smooth.

Season with salt to taste.

2 x 400g (14oz) cans butter (lima) beans, drained and rinsed

Generous handful of fresh flat-leaf parsley, finely chopped

Generous drizzle of extra virgin olive oil

Juice of 1 unwaxed lemon

Pinch of sea salt

3. garlic baguettes

It's often difficult to source vegan garlic bread in the supermarket, as many contain dairy. This is a simple recipe using shop-bought, part-baked baguettes and a homemade garlic butter.

Score the baguettes with a knife, leaving space at the bottom – that way the bread remains whole until it is shared at the table.

Preheat the oven to 200°C/400°F/gas mark 6. In a mixing bowl, combine the vegan butter, garlic, parsley and sea salt flakes until creamy.

Arrange the scored baguettes onto a baking tray, then use a teaspoon to push small amounts of the vegan butter between the slices of bread.

Wrap the baguettes in foil. Bake in for 5 minutes. Fold back the foil carefully and bake for a 4–5 minutes until golden. Drizzle with extra virgin olive oil and serve hot.

4 tbsp vegan butter, softened

2 cloves of garlic, crushed

Small handful of flat-leaf parsley, finely chopped

½ tsp sea salt flakes, crushed

2 part-baked white baguettes, scored into 8 slices for tearing

Drizzle of extra virgin olive oil

4. fennel and radicchio slaw

This fresh, fragrant, sweet and bitter slaw is the perfect side to the rich Chestnut mushroom bourguignon (page 38). It's simple to make, yet the flavours are complex enough to get everyone talking!

This slaw will keep for 2–3 days in an airtight container in the fridge.

Mix together the fennel and radicchio in a bowl.

Grate in the orange zest and squeeze over the orange juice, then stir through to combine.

Finish with a drizzle of smoked rapeseed oil and smoked sea salt.

1 head of fennel, finely sliced

1 head of radicchio, finely sliced

Zest and juice of 1 unwaxed orange

Generous drizzle of smoked extra virgin rapeseed oil

Generous pinch of smoked sea salt flakes, crushed

5. mint and mustard green beans

Brighten up your dinner table with these fresh and flavourful green beans.

This hot side dish also tastes excellent as a chilled salad.

Bring a saucepan of water to the boil over a high heat and throw in the green beans. Cook for 4–5 minutes until tender.

In the meantime, whisk together the olive oil, lemon juice and mustard until combined.

Drain the water from the green beans and pour over the dressing. Toss until all the green beans are coated.

Scatter with the mint leaves just before serving.

400g (14oz) green beans, ends trimmed

4 tbsp extra virgin olive oil

Juice of 1 unwaxed lemon

1 tsp Dijon mustard

Generous handful of fresh mint leaves, finely chopped

south asian supper

Serves 4

1. Garden biryani

2. Coconut, cucumber and garden mint raita

3. Bombay potatoes

4. Mango, radish and lime salsa

5. Naan chips

A flavourful feast full of comforting spices and textures. Pair with Masala chai (page 90) or a few cold beers.

I. garden biryani

Traditionally, biryani is slow-cooked, however, this version lends itself well to fast cooking due to the variety of rice used and the quick-cook vegetables. Adapt the vegetables to what you have available seasonally for an ever-changing dish.

Heat the sunflower oil in a large saucepan over a medium–high heat and cook the onion for 1 minute until it begins to soften. Add the cauliflower, green beans and yellow pepper, and sauté for 2–3 minutes.

Spoon in the curry paste, turmeric, cumin and chilli flakes, and stir to coat the vegetables.

Pour in the basmati rice and vegetable stock, then simmer over a medium heat for 9 minutes, stirring frequently.

Stir through the peas and cashew nuts, and cook for a further minute.

Remove from the heat and squeeze over the lemon juice. Scatter with the coriander, red chilli and sea salt just before serving.

1 tbsp sunflower oil

1 onion, finely chopped

½ small cauliflower, broken into florets

12 green beans, ends trimmed

1 yellow (bell) pepper, finely sliced

2 tbsp medium curry paste

1 tsp turmeric

1 tsp ground cumin

½ tsp dried chilli flakes

400g (14oz/2¼ cups) basmati rice

1 litre (1¾ pints/4½ cups) hot vegetable stock

2 tbsp frozen peas

2 tbsp roasted cashew nuts

Juice of 1 unwaxed lemon

Generous handful of fresh coriander (cilantro), roughly torn

1 red chilli, deseeded and finely sliced

Generous pinch of sea salt

social

2. coconut, cucumber and garden mint raita

Cooling and refreshing, this raita is a vital addition to any Indian-inspired meal and delicious served with Naan chips (page 49).

Spoon the coconut yoghurt into a large bowl.

Stir in the cucumber, mint and lime juice, and season with sea salt to taste.

8 tbsp chilled unsweetened coconut yoghurt

¼ cucumber, finely chopped

Handful of mint leaves, finely chopped

Juice of 1 unwaxed lime and pinch of sea salt

You can find many brands and varieties of coconut yoghurt in supermarkets and health food shops. I'd recommend choosing an unsweetened version for this recipe.

3. bombay potatoes

Here's a 15-minute spin on Bombay potatoes that makes them quick and effortless to make. Don't be afraid to use canned potatoes here – they've already been peeled, saving you time, and they absorb the flavours of the spices perfectly.

Thoroughly drain and rinse the potatoes before use.

Heat the sunflower oil in a frying pan over a medium–high heat for 2 minutes, then fry the mustard seeds until they start to brown. Stir in the turmeric, chilli powder, paprika and cardamom until combined into a hot, flavoured oil.

Carefully stir in the potatoes and coat in the oil. Cook for 5 minutes until the potatoes are hot, then remove from the heat.

Stir through the tomatoes and green chilli to coat in the oil mixture, then scatter with the coriander and sea salt just before serving.

3 tbsp sunflower oil

1 tsp mustard seeds

1 tsp turmeric

½ tsp chilli powder

½ tsp paprika

½ tsp ground cardamom

300g (10oz) can new potatoes, drained, rinsed and halved

6 ripe tomatoes, quartered

1 green chilli, deseeded and finely sliced

Small handful of fresh coriander (cilantro), roughly chopped

Pinch of sea salt

4. mango, radish and lime salsa

Sweet, fresh and the perfect accompaniment to any spiced dish.

———

This salsa will keep for 2–3 days in an airtight container in the fridge.

Combine the mango, radishes and parsley in a bowl. Squeeze over the lime juice and allow to stand for 10 minutes before serving.

1 medium mango, peeled and chopped into small chunks

6 radishes, quartered

Handful of fresh flat-leaf parsley

Juice of 1 unwaxed lime

5. naan chips

Hot, crispy and moreish, these naan chips are the perfect dipping partners to the Coconut, cucumber and garden mint raita (page 47).

———

Read the ingredients of shop-bought naan breads, as they may contain dairy products. Many supermarket-own brands are made without dairy.

Preheat the oven to 200°C/400°F/gas mark 6.

Place the naan triangles onto a baking tray, scatter with the chilli flakes and drizzle with olive oil.

Bake for 8–10 minutes until golden and crisp. Scatter with smoked sea salt just before serving.

6 naan breads (ensure milk free), cut into triangles

½ tsp dried chilli flakes

Generous drizzle of olive oil

Pinch of smoked sea salt

persian sharer

Serves 4

1. Aubergine, olive and butter bean cassoulet

2. Apricot, pistachio and mint pilaf

3. Grilled courgettes with dill yoghurt

4. Artichoke and pine nut orzo

5. Pan-fried crispy chickpeas

A vibrant spread with lots of enticing colours. It's easy to pull together – but very impressive to serve.

1. aubergine, olive and butter bean cassoulet

Aubergine soaks up the wonderful flavours of oregano and cinnamon in this moreish cassoulet. Serve straight to the table in its cooking pot for a simple, rustic meal. A true crowd-pleaser.

Heat the olive oil in a large saucepan over a high heat, then add the aubergine, oregano, mixed herbs and cinnamon. Cook for 3 minutes, stirring frequently.

Add the onion and red pepper, and cook for a further 2 minutes until the onion begins to soften.

Pour in the chopped tomatoes, 150ml (5¼fl oz/⅔ cup) of water and ketchup, followed by the olives and butter beans. Reduce the heat to medium, partially cover with a lid and simmer for 10 minutes, stirring occasionally.

Scatter with the parsley and season with sea salt just before serving.

2 tbsp olive oil

1 large aubergine (eggplant), cut into even bite-sized cubes

1 tsp dried oregano

1 tsp dried mixed herbs

½ tsp ground cinnamon

1 red onion, finely diced

1 red (bell) pepper, sliced

400g (14oz) can chopped tomatoes

1 tbsp tomato ketchup

2 tbsp green olives

400g (14oz) can butter (lima) beans, drained and rinsed

Handful of fresh flat-leaf parsley, roughly chopped

Pinch of sea salt

2. apricot, pistachio and mint pilaf

This simple and beautiful pilaf uses bulgur wheat as a base, with a flavour twist on the traditional side salad, tabbouleh. Sweet dried apricots, fragrant pistachios and refreshing mint are brought together with lemon juice to create the perfect sharing side dish.

Save time by chopping the herbs, pistachios and apricots while the bulgur wheat is soaking.

Place the bulgur wheat into a small bowl and pour over enough boiling-hot water to cover. Place a plate over the bowl to form a seal and to aid absorption of the water into the wheat. Leave to stand for 10 minutes.

Spoon the bulgur wheat into a mixing bowl and stir in the mint, parsley, apricots and pistachios.

Stir through the extra virgin olive oil and lemon slices, then sprinkle through the sea salt. Mix until combined.

100g (3½oz/¾ cup) bulgur wheat

Generous handful of fresh mint leaves, finely chopped

Generous handful of fresh flat-leaf parsley, finely chopped

15 soft dried apricots, finely chopped

3 tbsp shelled pistachios, roughly chopped

Generous drizzle of extra virgin olive oil

1 unwaxed lemon, sliced

Generous pinch of sea salt

3. grilled courgettes with dill yoghurt

This plate of hot, charred courgettes is a versatile side dish, but also works well as a large salad plate when served over crisp leaves. Keep the yoghurt chilled until serving to best appreciate the contrast between the hot courgettes and the cool, herbed yoghurt.

―――――――

Heat the griddle pan over a high heat while you prepare the courgettes to achieve the optimum grilling temperature.

Heat a griddle pan over a high heat while you brush the courgette strips with olive oil. Place the strips onto the hot pan and cook for 3–4 minutes until defined 'charred' lines begin to show. Flip the courgettes over and cook on the other side for 3–4 minutes.

In the meantime, make the yoghurt dressing. Combine the soya yoghurt, dill, lemon juice and sea salt in a small bowl, and chill until ready to serve.

When the courgettes are grilled on both sides, arrange them on a serving plate and scatter with the capers. Generously spoon over the yoghurt dressing just before serving.

4 medium courgettes (zucchini), sliced into long 2cm (¾in) thick strips

Drizzle of extra virgin olive oil

4 rounded tbsp unsweetened soya yoghurt

1 tbsp fresh dill, finely chopped

Juice of ½ unwaxed lemon

Pinch of sea salt

1 tsp capers, drained of brine or oil

4. artichoke and pine nut orzo

If you need inspiration to use up that jar of oil-preserved artichokes sitting at the back of your fridge, this is the recipe for you.

Orzo is a rice-shaped pasta found in most supermarkets. Check that it is egg free, but most varieties tend to be.

Bring a medium pan of water to the boil over a medium heat and add the orzo pasta. Cook for 7–8 minutes until al dente.

In the meantime, toast the pine nuts in a dry pan for 2–3 minutes until golden, then set aside.

In a bowl, whisk together the olive oil, cider vinegar, lemon zest and juice. Season the dressing with sea salt and black pepper to taste.

Drain the water thoroughly from the orzo. Stir through the artichokes and pour over the dressing. Stir well to combine.

Scatter with the toasted pine nuts before serving.

300g (10oz/2 cups) dried orzo pasta (ensure egg free)

4 tbsp pine nuts

4 tbsp extra virgin olive oil

1 tsp cider vinegar

Zest and juice of 1 unwaxed lemon

Generous pinch of sea salt and black pepper

4 jarred grilled artichokes in oil, drained and roughly chopped

5. pan-fried crispy chickpeas

These crispy chickpeas are a delicious amuse-bouche to this menu, or a moreish snack any time of the day.

———

The cooked chickpeas will last for up to 4 days in an airtight container.

Heat the olive oil in a large frying pan over a medium heat and cook the chickpeas for 10 minutes until they start to become crispy.

Scatter over the smoked paprika, chilli flakes, cumin and sea salt, and stir through for 2 minutes.

Remove from the heat and allow to cool for a couple of minutes before serving.

4 tbsp olive oil

400g (14oz) can chickpeas, drained and rinsed

1 tbsp smoked paprika

1 tsp dried chilli flakes

½ tsp ground cumin

Pinch of sea salt

thai feast

Serves 4

1. Soy-glazed butternut thai green curry

2. Spicy peanut sauce

3. Ginger, sesame and lime glass noodles

4. Quick pickled radishes

5. Green tea and coconut rice

A vibrant and punchy meal for any time of the year – the accompaniments make this a wonderful sharing feast, but the curry on its own also works well.

1. soy-glazed butternut thai green curry

Creamy, delicately spiced Thai-style curry is a crowd-pleaser, and is best shared. Never think less of shop-bought curry pastes, they are simply a concentrated spice mix. Check that the curry paste is vegan, as some contain fish sauce.

To make chopping a butternut squash easier, simply blast it in the microwave for a couple of minutes to soften.

Heat the sunflower oil in a wok while you dip the butternut squash cubes into the soy sauce. Add the soy-coated butternut squash to the wok and cook over a medium–high heat for 10 minutes until softened and browned, stirring frequently.

Move on to the Thai green curry base. Heat the sunflower oil in a separate large frying pan. Add the lemongrass and Thai green curry paste, and infuse over a high heat for 1 minute. Stir in the coconut milk, then reduce the heat slightly

and simmer for 8 minutes. Remove and discard the lemongrass stalk.

Throw the sugar snap peas, asparagus spears, green beans and edamame beans into the curry sauce and cook for 4–5 minutes until the vegetables are al dente.

Ladle the curry into bowls and spoon in the softened soy-glazed butternut squash. Top each bowl with a squeeze of lime juice, sprinkle with the coriander, add a few slices of chilli and a scattering of spring onion.

For the soy-glazed butternut squash
2 tbsp sunflower oil

1 medium butternut squash, peeled and cut into bite-sized cubes

3 tbsp light soy sauce

For the Thai green curry base
1 tbsp sunflower oil

1 stalk of lemongrass, bruised

2 tbsp Thai green curry paste (ensure fish free)

2 x 400ml (14fl oz) cans full-fat coconut milk

Handful of sugar snap peas, halved

Handful of asparagus spears, tough ends removed

Handful of green beans, ends trimmed

2 tbsp frozen or fresh edamame beans

Juice of 1 unwaxed lime, plus fresh wedges for serving

Generous handful of fresh coriander (cilantro), roughly torn

1 red chilli, deseeded and finely sliced

1 spring onion (scallion), finely chopped

2. spicy peanut sauce

No Thai-style feast would be complete without a spicy peanut sauce. Spoon over noodles or simply serve as a dip for guests to tuck into.

Heat the sunflower oil in a frying pan and add the chilli flakes. Infuse over a medium–high heat for 1–2 minutes.

Reduce the heat to low–medium and spoon in the peanut butter. Pour in 100ml (3½fl oz/scant ½ cup) cold water and use a balloon whisk to beat until smooth.

Stir through the spring onion and soy sauce.

2 tsp sunflower oil

1 tsp dried chilli flakes

4 rounded tbsp smooth peanut butter

1 spring onion (scallion), finely chopped

1 tbsp dark soy sauce

3. ginger, sesame and lime glass noodles

Glass noodles are often made with mung beans or other starches to create an almost clear, slippery noodle. This dish is simple, moreish and fresh. Delicious alone, but even better as part of this Thai feast.

———

Look for glass noodles in the supermarket world food aisle, or buy them from a local Chinese supermarket.

Soak the noodles in boiling water for 5 minutes, or as per packet instructions.

Heat the sunflower oil in a wok over a high heat until smoking, then throw in the chilli, cinnamon, ginger and spring onions, and stir-fry for 1 minute.

Add in the sugar snap peas, beansprouts and soy sauce, and stir-fry for 2 minutes. Drain the water from the noodles and separate them into the wok, coating them in the infused oil for 2 minutes until piping hot.

Remove from the heat and stir through the lime juice. Scatter with the sesame seeds and coriander. Serve immediately.

300g (10oz) dried glass noodles

1 tbsp sunflower oil

1 red chilli, deseeded and finely chopped

Pinch of ground cinnamon

2cm (¾in) piece of ginger, peeled and grated

2 spring onions (scallions), finely chopped

Handful of sugar snap peas

Generous handful of fresh beansprouts

1 tbsp light soy sauce

Juice of 1 unwaxed lime

2 tbsp sesame seeds

Handful of fresh coriander (cilantro), roughly torn

4. quick pickled radishes

I love the tang of these pickled radishes that cut through the creaminess of coconut-based curries. No one will ever believe they're ready to eat in less than 15 minutes!

Put the radishes and spring onion into a small jar or small bowl.

Spoon over the rice vinegar and maple syrup, then stir in the chilli flakes, coriander and sea salt. Allow to infuse for 10 minutes before serving.

10 radishes, very finely sliced

1 spring onion (scallion), finely sliced

5 tbsp rice vinegar

1 tsp maple syrup

½ tsp dried chilli flakes

Small handful of fresh coriander (cilantro), finely chopped

Pinch of sea salt

5. green tea and coconut rice

Serve clouds of this creamy, fragrant rice as a simple side dish.

Heat the creamed coconut in a saucepan over a medium heat, then add the rice and stir through to coat the grains.

Pour in the hot green tea, stir and loosely cover with a lid. Cook for 10–12 minutes until the liquid has been absorbed and the rice is plump. Season with sea salt to taste.

200g (7oz/⅔ cup) creamed coconut

350g (12oz/2 cups) basmati rice

600ml (1 pint/2½ cups) green tea made with boiling water and a tea bag, or tea leaves discarded after brewing

Pinch of sea salt

tex-mex fiesta

Serves 4

1. Fajita casserole crush

2. Beetroot guacamole

3. Creamed corn

4. Salsa pinwheels

5. Refried beans

This Mexican meal is a real people-pleaser – it looks bright and cheerful on the table and is super simple to make.

I. fajita casserole crush

Cook this fun casserole in a stove-to-table dish and get everyone stuck in! Spoon through layers of crispy tortillas, smooth avocado and spicy beans and peppers.

Preheat the oven to 200°C/400°F/gas mark 6.

Arrange the tortilla triangles on a baking tray and drizzle with the olive oil. Bake for 8–10 minutes until golden.

In the meantime, heat the sunflower oil in a large stove-to-table casserole dish over a medium–high heat and cook the onion and red and yellow peppers for 2–3 minutes until they begin to soften, then add the green beans, chilli powder, smoked paprika, garlic powder and cumin, and cook for a further minute.

Add the yeast extract, kidney beans and passata, and bubble for 10 minutes until the vegetables have softened.

Remove from the heat and scatter over the cherry tomatoes, avocado, onion and green chilli. Squeeze over the lime juice.

Gently scatter with the baked tortilla chips and coriander, and season with smoked sea salt to taste.

2 soft tortillas, cut into triangles

1 tbsp olive oil

1 tbsp sunflower oil

1 onion, roughly sliced

1 red (bell) pepper, roughly sliced

1 yellow (bell) pepper, sliced

Small handful of green beans

1 tsp chilli powder

1 tsp smoked paprika

½ tsp garlic powder

½ tsp ground cumin

1 tsp yeast extract

400g (14oz) can red kidney beans, drained and rinsed

300g (10oz/1¼ cups) passata

6 cherry tomatoes, halved

1 avocado, finely chopped

1 small red onion, finely sliced

1 small green chilli, finely sliced

Juice of 1 unwaxed lime

Generous handful of fresh coriander (cilantro), roughly torn

Generous pinch of smoked sea salt

2. beetroot guacamole

Give guacamole a colourful twist with beetroot. Earthy, chunky and perfect for sharing.

———

Cooked beetroot can be found in supermarket salad fridges, which saves on long roasting times.

In a bowl, use a fork to crush the avocados until semi-smooth.

Stir through the spring onion, beetroots and coriander, then squeeze through the lime juice. Season with salt to taste.

If you prefer a silky smooth dip, blitz all of the ingredients in a blender.

2 ripe avocados, peeled and stones removed

1 spring onion (scallion), finely sliced

2 small cooked beetroots, diced

Generous handful of fresh coriander (cilantro), finely chopped

Juice of 1 unwaxed lime

Generous pinch of smoked sea salt

social

3. creamed corn

Usually, corn is creamed using the milky liquid that is collected from the cob when slicing away the corn. This traditional method can be time consuming, so I've created this speedy version, which is ready in under 10 minutes.

—

If using sweetcorn from the freezer, it can be cooked from frozen. If you're using canned sweetcorn, thoroughly drain and rinse away the salted water from the can.

Heat the soya milk and vegan butter in a saucepan until combined, whisking gently.

Spoon in the sweetcorn and cook for 8 minutes until simmering.

Remove from the heat and use a hand blender to purée half of the mixture. Then stir through the sea salt. Scatter with the nutmeg and serve hot.

150ml (5¼ fl oz/generous ½ cup) unsweetened soya milk

1 rounded tbsp vegan butter

8 rounded tbsp frozen or canned sweetcorn

Pinch of sea salt

Pinch of freshly grated nutmeg

4. salsa pinwheels

These simple pastry pinwheels are perfect for sharing, as they look impressive but take just minutes to make.

Serve any excess salsa in a bowl with the Beetroot guacamole (page 70) for a perfect balance of fiery and cooling.

Preheat the oven to 200°C/400°F/gas mark 6.

In a bowl, mix together the tomatoes, onion, chilli, coriander and lime juice. Season with sea salt.

Arrange the pastry sheet on a level surface. Evenly spread over the salsa, then roll the pastry into a log shape. Use a sharp knife to cut 12 even slices.

Arrange the slices cut-side down on a baking tray, then use a pastry brush to glaze them with a little soya milk. Bake for 10–12 minutes until golden.

150g (5½oz) tomatoes, finely chopped

1 small red onion, finely chopped

1 red chilli, finely chopped

Handful of fresh coriander (cilantro), finely chopped

Juice of 1 unwaxed lime

Pinch of sea salt

1 sheet of pre-rolled puff pastry (ensure dairy free)

2 tsp soya milk, for glazing

5. refried beans

It wouldn't be a Tex-Mex feast without refried beans. Proper comfort food for everyone to enjoy together.

Heat the sunflower oil in a large saucepan over a medium–high heat and cook the onion for 3 minutes until softened. Add the chipotle paste, paprika, cinnamon and garlic powder, and stir through for 1 minute.

Tip in the borlotti beans and black beans, and reduce the heat to low–medium, stirring frequently for 8 minutes.

When the beans are heated, use a potato masher to smooth through the beans. Squeeze over the lime juice and season with smoked sea salt. Serve hot.

1 tbsp sunflower oil

1 red onion, finely sliced

1 tsp chipotle paste

1 tsp paprika

½ tsp ground cinnamon

½ tsp garlic powder

400g (14oz) can borlotti beans, drained and rinsed

400g (14oz) can black beans, drained and rinsed

Juice of ½ unwaxed lime

Generous pinch of smoked sea salt

solo

Sometimes, you just need to throw on a jumper and put your feet up with a bowl of comfort food for one. Unapologetic indulgence, simple pleasures and finger-licking food – it doesn't get any better than this. In this chapter, you'll find a main dish and an accompanying side dish because more is wonderfully more, when you're eating alone.

breakfast sundae

Serves 1

A breakfast that looks like pudding is an excellent start to the day.

Mix together the oats, pumpkin seeds and pecans in a small bowl.

In a glass, arrange the oat mixture in layers with the soya yoghurt, strawberries, raspberries and grapes.

Serve immediately so that the oats remain crisp.

2 tbsp rolled oats

1 tsp pumpkin seeds

1 tsp pecan nuts, chopped roughly

3 tbsp vanilla soya yoghurt

2 strawberries, hulled and roughly chopped

2 raspberries, halved

2 red grapes, halved

breakfast hash

Serves 1

Start the day the comforting way with this one-pan breakfast.

Heat the olive oil in a frying pan over a medium–high heat and add the potato. Cook for 10 minutes, turning frequently until golden brown.

Throw in the mushrooms and cherry tomatoes, and cook for 3 minutes until softened. Add the spinach and cook for a minute.

Sprinkle with Tabasco sauce to taste. Then arrange over the avocado and chilli.

2 tbsp olive oil

1 waxy potato (such as Maris Piper), peeled and evenly diced

6 button mushrooms, cleaned

6 cherry tomatoes

Generous handful of spinach

Few drops of Tabasco sauce

1 avocado, stoned, peeled and sliced

½ red chilli, deseeded and finely sliced

french onion soup

Serves 1

Everyday ingredients come together brilliantly in this classic French soup. And yeast extract offers a deeper, more savoury stock to contrast the sweet onions.

Heat the olive oil in a large saucepan over a medium heat and cook the onions for 5 minutes until softened. Add the sugar and thyme, and cook for 5–6 minutes until caramelised. Add the garlic and cook for 1 minute.

Add the red wine, vegetable stock and yeast extract to a separate pan. Simmer over a medium heat for 10 minutes.

Pour the hot stock mixture over the caramelised onions and simmer for 1 minute. Season to taste.

1 tbsp olive oil

3 onions, finely sliced

2 tsp soft brown sugar

1 tsp dried thyme

2 cloves of garlic, crushed

100ml (3½fl oz/scant ½ cup) red wine (ensure vegan)

500ml (17½fl oz/2 cups) hot vegetable stock

1 tsp yeast extract

Generous pinch of sea salt and black pepper

parsley toasts

Serves 1

Fragrant toasts make a delightful dipping partner to the French onion soup.

Preheat the oven to 180°C/350°F/gas mark 4. Arrange the baguette slices on a baking tray and rub with the garlic clove. Drizzle with olive oil and bake for 5–6 minutes until toasted.

Spread mustard over half of each slice, then sprinkle some parsley over this half (the other half stays plain).

4 thick slices of white baguette

1 clove of garlic, peeled

Generous drizzle of olive oil

½ tsp Dijon mustard

Small handful of fresh flat-leaf parsley, finely chopped

spaghetti alla puttanesca

Serves 1 generously

I first came across this classic Italian dish in *Nigella's Kitchen* cookbook. Traditionally, the sauce contains anchovies, however, the olives and capers add all the saltiness it needs to be seasoned and addictive. All the ingredients are found in the storecupboard, making this the ultimate convenient, fast and seductive bowl of pasta.

Heat the olive oil in a large saucepan over a medium heat and cook the garlic for 1 minute until softened. Sprinkle in the chilli flakes and oregano, along with the capers and olives, and allow them to infuse in the oil for a further minute.

Pour in the passata and stir through the sugar to balance the acidity. Loosely cover with a lid and allow to simmer for 10 minutes.

In the meantime, cook the spaghetti in boiling water in a separate pan for 9–10 minutes until al dente.

Drain the water from the pan and toss the spaghetti into the sauce until coated. Remove from the heat and season with sea salt and black pepper to taste. Serve immediately.

1 tbsp olive oil

2 cloves of garlic, crushed

½ tsp dried chilli flakes

½ tsp dried oregano

2 tsp capers, drained of oil or brine

5 black olives, pitted and halved

250g (9oz/1 cup) passata

1 tsp caster (superfine) sugar

100g (3½oz) dried spaghetti (ensure egg free)

Sea salt and black pepper

heritage tomato and toasted pine nut salad

Serves 1 generously

One of my earliest memories is watering tomato plants in my dad's greenhouse. I loved having soil on my fingers and watching how the magic of light turned the seeds into plump, imperfect fruits. To this day, I can't walk past vine tomatoes without finding the need to deeply inhale the fresh, green scent that takes me back to that greenhouse in my childhood garden.

Heritage tomatoes are the star of this simple salad, which pairs perfectly with Spaghetti alla puttanesca (page 78).

Add the pine nuts to a dry pan and toast over a medium heat for 1–2 minutes until golden, then set aside.

Combine the tomatoes, rocket and extra virgin olive oil, and season with black pepper to taste.

Scatter over the toasted pine nuts just before serving.

1 rounded tbsp pine nuts

200g (7oz) mixed heritage tomatoes, roughly chopped

Small handful of rocket (arugula)

3 rounded tbsp good-quality extra virgin olive oil

Pinch of black pepper

grapefruit gremolata

Makes 1 small bowl

As winter becomes spring, brighten slow-cooked dishes such as tagines and Bolognese with a sprinkle of gremolata. It's zesty, fresh and unexpected with bitter grapefruit. Delicious sprinkled over Red bean goulash (page 29).

Combine all the ingredients in a bowl and allow the flavours to infuse for at least 10 minutes.

Small handful of fresh flat-leaf parsley, finely chopped

2 cloves of garlic, grated

Zest of 1 unwaxed grapefruit, coarsely grated

sweet potato and cinnamon latkes

Serves 1

These latkes have a crisp, caramelised outer and a sweet potato centre, making them the most perfect comfort food. Latkes are traditionally served over Jewish holiday celebrations, bringing memories of family, home and happiness to anyone eating them. This version uses sweet potatoes and cinnamon to add a flavour twist that is perfect for anyone trying these delights for the first time.

Vegan cream cheese is now readily available in large supermarkets, often with a choice of brands and flavour maturity. Serve it cool and generously over these latkes.

Put the grated sweet potato and red onion into a clean, dry tea towel and squeeze out as much liquid as possible.

Add the drained sweet potato and red onion to a medium bowl and stir in the flour, cinnamon, smoked paprika and salt until the strands are coated.

Heat the sunflower oil in a frying pan over a medium heat while you shape the latkes into small, flat patties. Test that the oil is ready by adding in a couple of shreds of sweet potato – they should gently sizzle.

Carefully add the latkes and cook for 3–4 minutes on each side until golden brown.

While the latkes are cooking, mix the vegan cream cheese and dill together in a small bowl. Carefully remove the latkes from the pan and drain on kitchen paper. Serve hot with lashings of vegan cream cheese and dill.

1 medium sweet potato, peeled and coarsely grated

1 small red onion, coarsely grated

2 tsp plain (all-purpose) flour

Pinch of ground cinnamon

Pinch of smoked paprika

Generous pinch of sea salt

4 tbsp sunflower oil

2 rounded tbsp vegan cream cheese

1 tbsp finely chopped fresh dill

orange, carrot and sultana pearl couscous

Serves 1 generously

Pearl or giant couscous has a light texture and is less grainy than its miniature counterpart. This salad can be served hot or chilled and will last for a couple of days in the fridge.

———

Experiment with various coloured carrots as the seasons allow. Purple carrots really brighten up this dish!

Add the pearl couscous, sultanas and fresh orange juice to a small saucepan and simmer over a medium heat for 10 minutes until the orange juice has been absorbed.

Remove from the heat and stir through the carrot, orange zest and coriander. Season with sea salt to taste.

40g (1¼oz/¼ cup) pearl couscous

1 tbsp golden sultanas (golden raisins)

100ml (3½fl oz/scant ½ cup) fresh orange juice

1 small carrot, coarsely grated

Zest of 1 unwaxed orange

Handful of fresh coriander (cilantro), finely chopped
Pinch of sea salt

double-decker spicy falafel burger

Serves 1

There are times when you need more than a bite-sized falafel in a flatbread. Those times call for thick, spicy burgers layered with onion and houmous in a toasted, seeded bun. There's no need for manners here, just get stuck in!

To make the burgers, add the chickpeas, cumin, smoked paprika, chilli flakes, coriander, parsley and harissa to a high-powered blender or food processor and blitz until semi-smooth. Leave some chunks to add some bite.

Carefully remove the mixture from the blender or food processor and shape into two flat burgers.

Mix the breadcrumbs and sesame seeds onto a saucer and gently press the burgers into them.

Heat the sunflower oil in a frying pan over a medium–high heat until hot. Carefully add the burgers to the pan and cook for 4–5 minutes on each side until golden.

In the meantime, heat a dry griddle pan over a high heat and toast the bread bun for 2 minutes. Remove from the heat and layer the lettuce onto one half of the bun.

Place the first burger onto the lettuce and spoon on the houmous and onion rings, then add the second burger and chutney. Top with the other bun half. Serve immediately.

For the burgers
400g (14oz) can chickpeas, drained and rinsed

2 rounded tsp ground cumin

½ tsp smoked paprika

½ tsp dried chilli flakes

2 handfuls of fresh coriander (cilantro) with stalks

1 handful of fresh flat-leaf parsley with stalks

1 tsp harissa paste

1 slice of white bread, grated into breadcrumbs

1 tbsp sesame seeds

4 tbsp sunflower oil

For the additions
1 large seeded white bread bun, halved

½ baby gem lettuce, tough stems discarded and roughly sliced

1 tbsp houmous

4 red onion rings

1 tbsp Cheat's apricot and fig chutney (page 86)

solo

cheat's apricot and fig chutney

Makes 1 small jar

This 10-minute chutney is delicious served with my Double-decker spicy falafel burger (page 84), but equally excellent loaded into a baguette for lunch. Allow to cool and keep refrigerated in a clean, airtight jar for up to 5 days.

Add the dried apricots, figs, apricot jam, cider vinegar, Chinese five spice and chilli flakes to a medium saucepan and simmer over a low–medium heat for 10 minutes.

Remove from the heat and season with sea salt and black pepper to taste.

10 soft dried apricots, roughly chopped

3 soft dried figs, finely chopped

6 rounded tbsp apricot jam

1 tsp cider vinegar

Pinch of Chinese five spice

Pinch of dried chilli flakes

Pinch of sea salt and black pepper

charred pepper tacos

Serves 1

Hot, crunchy and charred, these tacos are the ultimate comfort food for one. I've allowed for two tacos, but load more if you feel extra hungry or inclined. Best served with Saffron rice (page 88).

––––––

You can find dairy-free soured cream in many supermarket free-from sections. If you don't have any to hand, simply stir a squeeze of lemon juice and sea salt into 2 tablespoons of unsweetened soya yoghurt.

Heat the sunflower oil in a griddle pan over a medium–high heat until smoking hot. Throw in the peppers and char for 3–4 minutes without stirring. Then stir through and allow to char for a further 2–3 minutes.

Remove from the heat and squeeze over the lime juice. Scatter with the chilli, parsley and smoked sea salt.

Load into the taco shells and generously spoon over the vegan soured cream.

1 tsp sunflower oil

1 red (bell) pepper, deseeded and roughly sliced

1 yellow (bell) pepper, deseeded and roughly sliced

1 green (bell) pepper, deseeded and roughly sliced

Juice of 1 unwaxed lime

1 red chilli, deseeded and finely sliced

Small handful of fresh flat-leaf parsley, roughly chopped

Generous pinch of smoked sea salt

2 corn taco shells

2 tbsp vegan soured cream

saffron rice

Serves 1

Vibrant and precious, saffron infuses the basmati rice to give a flowery, honeyed fragrance with a gently sweet, spiced flavour.

Saffron is expensive, however, it keeps well in a cool, dark cupboard.

Add the rice, saffron threads, cinnamon stick, cardamom pods and star anise to a saucepan with 250ml (8¾fl oz/1 cup) of cold water, and bring to the boil over a high heat. Reduce the heat and simmer for 12–13 minutes until the liquid has been absorbed.

Remove the cinnamon stick, cardamom pods and star anise and discard. Add the sultanas and pistachios and stir to combine.

Drizzle with extra virgin olive oil and season with sea salt to taste.

100g (3½oz/½ cup) basmati rice, rinsed

Pinch of saffron threads

1 cinnamon stick

2 cardamom pods

1 star anise

1 tsp plump sultanas (golden raisins)

1 tsp pistachios, shelled and halved

Drizzle of extra virgin olive oil

Pinch of sea salt

masala
chai

This milky, sweet tea is the perfect comforting drink to have with Spiced beans on toast (opposite). I love the rich taste of oat milk in this version, perfect when combined with the sweet spices. Deliciously hot, frothy and sweet.

Pour the oat milk and 100ml (3½fl oz/scant ½ cup) of cold water into a medium saucepan. Add the cardamom pods, peppercorns, clove, cinnamon stick and sugar, then simmer over a medium heat for 10 minutes.

Remove from the heat and add the tea bag. Stir and cover with a lid. Allow to infuse for 2 minutes.

Drain the tea through a strainer into a mug or warmed tea pot, and serve.

200ml (7fl oz/generous ¾ cup) oat milk

3 green cardamom pods

2 black peppercorns

1 clove

1 cinnamon stick

2 tsp caster (superfine) sugar

1 English breakfast tea bag

spiced beans on toast

Serves 1

In times of need, I love eating beans on toast. The humble can of baked beans transforms toast into something nostalgic and comforting. This version combines garlic and Indian-style spices with a fresh hit of lemon to take beans on toast to another level.

Heat the sunflower oil in a saucepan over a medium heat and cook the garlic, spring onion, chilli flakes, garam masala and cumin for 2 minutes until the garlic softens.

Pour in the baked beans, including the tomato sauce, and reduce the heat to low. Simmer for 5 minutes, stirring frequently to combine everything in the pan and avoid sticking.

In the meantime, toast the bread until golden.

When the beans are piping hot, scatter over the coriander and squeeze in the lemon juice. Season with sea salt to taste. Spoon the beans and sauce over the toast and serve immediately.

2 tsp sunflower oil

1 clove of garlic, crushed

1 spring onion (scallion), finely chopped

½ tsp dried chilli flakes

¼ tsp garam masala

Pinch of ground cumin

415g (14½oz) can baked beans in tomato sauce

2 slices of thick white bread

Small handful of fresh coriander (cilantro), roughly chopped

Juice of ½ unwaxed lemon

Pinch of sea salt

spicy beer-battered cauliflower wings

Serves 1 generously

If you need something quick, spicy and finger-licking, grab yourself a plate of these spicy beer-battered cauliflower 'wings'. The beer provides a light, crispy batter and works perfectly with the spices. Best served with the Trio of dips (opposite).

Cook the cauliflower wings in small batches of 2 or 3 to avoid them sticking to the pan and each other!

Heat the sunflower oil in a deep saucepan over a medium heat. In a large bowl, mix together the flour, cornflour, garlic powder, chilli powder, paprika and salt. Pour in the beer and use a balloon whisk to beat into a smooth batter. Dip the cauliflower florets in the batter and coat fully.

Test that the oil is hot enough by dripping in some of the batter. It should become golden brown within 5 seconds and gently rise to the surface.

Carefully drop 2 or 3 pieces of batter-coated cauliflower into the hot oil. Cook for 3–4 minutes until golden, turning as necessary.

Use a slotted spoon to remove the cauliflower from the pan, and drain on kitchen paper while you cook the remaining cauliflower. Serve warm.

500ml (17½fl oz/2 cups) sunflower oil, for frying

100g (3½oz/¾ cup) plain (all-purpose) flour

2 tbsp cornflour (cornstarch)

½ tsp garlic powder

1 tsp chilli powder

1 tsp paprika

Pinch of salt

300ml (½ pint/1¼ cups) chilled beer (ensure vegan)

½ head of cauliflower, broken into bite-sized florets

trio of dips

Serves 1

When you need a taster of everything, these dips will cool, excite and zing up your Spicy beer-battered cauliflower wings (opposite).

Egg-free vegan mayonnaise is readily available in supermarket free-from sections, as well as health food shops.

For the maple and soy dip: Whisk together the maple syrup, soy sauce and Worcestershire sauce and pour into a small serving bowl.

For the lemon mayo dip: Finely grate the lemon zest into the vegan mayonnaise and squeeze in the lemon juice. Combine fully and season with sea salt to taste.

For the spicy tomato dip: Mix together the ketchup, harissa and hot sauce until combined. Pour into a small serving dish.

For the maple and soy dip
2 tbsp maple syrup

1 tbsp dark soy sauce

2–3 drops vegan Worcestershire sauce (ensure anchovy free)

For the lemon mayo dip
Zest of ½ unwaxed lemon

2 tbsp vegan mayonnaise

1 tbsp lemon juice

Pinch of sea salt

For the spicy tomato dip
3 tbsp tomato ketchup

½ tsp harissa paste

2–3 drops hot sauce

cashew
chow mein

Serves 1

Before you order that takeaway for one, consider this storecupboard chow mein, ready in under 10 minutes with minimal preparation. It will become your go-to 'fakeaway' dish.

———

Tenderstem broccoli requires minimal preparation, as all of the vegetable can be eaten. If you don't have it available, use regular broccoli, with the tough stem trimmed, or switch for a handful of sugar snap peas.

Heat the sunflower oil in a wok over a high heat until hot. Throw in the ginger, garlic and spring onion, and stir-fry for 1 minute to infuse the oil.

Throw in the broccoli and cashew nuts, and stir-fry for 1 minute.

Pour in the soy sauce, sesame oil, Chinese five spice and sugar, and stir-fry for 2 minutes.

Add the noodles, separating them gently, then stir to coat the noodles in the sauce. Cook for a further 2 minutes until the noodles are piping hot, then remove from the heat.

Scatter with the sesame seeds and radishes, and serve immediately.

1 tbsp sunflower oil

1cm (½in) piece of ginger, peeled and grated

1 clove of garlic, finely sliced

1 spring onion (scallion), finely sliced

4 florets of tenderstem broccoli

Handful of cashew nuts

3 tbsp dark soy sauce

1 tsp toasted sesame oil

½ tsp Chinese five spice

Pinch of caster (superfine) sugar

150g (5½oz) straight-to-wok noodles (ensure egg free)

½ tsp sesame seeds

2 radishes, finely sliced

hazelnut-fried edamame beans

Serves 1 as a side dish

These quick and delicious beans make the perfect side dish to Cashew chow mein (page 94). Frozen edamame beans are a handy ingredient to keep in your freezer for a fast addition to any salad, stir-fry or casserole.

———

To defrost frozen edamame beans, simply soak in boiling water for 3–4 minutes.

Toast the hazelnuts in a dry frying pan over a medium heat until golden, then remove from the pan and set aside.

Heat the olive oil in the same pan over a medium–high heat, then add the chilli flakes and stir in the edamame beans. Toss in the oil for 2 minutes.

Remove from the heat and squeeze over the lime juice. Stir through the toasted hazelnuts and season with sea salt. Serve immediately.

1 tbsp chopped and blanched hazelnuts

2 tsp olive oil

½ tsp dried chilli flakes

5 rounded tbsp edamame beans, shelled and defrosted if frozen

Juice of ½ unwaxed lime

Generous pinch of sea salt flakes

marbled balsamic croutons

Serves 1

These tangy and crisp croutons are wonderful scattered over Risotto caprese (page 98) or to add crunch to a steamy bowl of soup. Great for using up stale bread (even the crust works well).

These croutons will last for 3 to 4 days in a sealed container, stored somewhere dark and cool.

Pour the olive oil onto a plate and drip over the balsamic vinegar. Use a fork to swirl the vinegar through the oil.

Begin to heat a dry frying pan over a medium–high heat while you dip the bread cubes into the oil mixture, allowing it to soak through.

Carefully place the bread cubes onto the hot pan and cook for 5–6 minutes, moving and tossing them frequently. Cook for a further 2 minutes over a high heat until golden and crisp. Serve immediately.

3 tbsp olive oil

2 tsp balsamic vinegar

1 slice of day-old white bread, cut into small, even cubes

risotto
caprese

Serves 1 generously

The magical results of this less-than-15-minute risotto are created in a pressure cooker. In what can take up to 30 minutes of cooking and laborious stirring, risotto can be high maintenance and definitely not a recipe for a 15-minute time slot – until you've tried this recipe. There's no peeking allowed once the pressure is set, so ensure your liquid volumes are exact in this trusted recipe.

———

Vegan cream cheese can be found in many supermarkets and health food shops. Experiment with plain, herbed or chilli-flavoured varieties!

Add the olive oil and onion to a pressure cooker over a medium–high heat, and soften the onion for 2–3 minutes, without the lid on at this stage.

Add the oregano and rice, and coat fully in the onion mixture until the edges of the rice become transparent, stirring constantly.

Pour in the wine and simmer for 2–3 minutes until absorbed.

Pour in the vegetable stock and stir through, then close the lid on the pressure cooker. Bring the pan up to high pressure and cook for 5 minutes, then release the pressure quickly, as per the manufacturer's instructions.

Reduce the heat to low and stir through the sundried tomatoes, cherry tomatoes and black olives, heating them through for 1 minute.

Serve in a large bowl and spoon over the vegan cream cheese, pushing teaspoon-sized amounts into the rice, allowing it to gently melt through.

Scatter with the basil leaves and season with sea salt and black pepper to taste.

2 tbsp olive oil

1 onion, finely chopped

1 tsp dried oregano

100g (3½oz/½ cup)
arborio rice

100ml (3½fl oz/scant ½ cup)
white wine (ensure vegan)

200ml (7fl oz/generous ¾ cup)
hot vegetable stock

6 soft sundried tomatoes,
drained of oil and roughly
chopped

4 cherry tomatoes, halved

4 black olives, pitted and halved

6 tsp vegan cream cheese

Generous handful of fresh basil
leaves, torn

Pinch of sea salt and black
pepper

jerk pulled pineapple

Serves 1 generously

The ultimate food to be enjoyed alone. These wraps are filled with spicy and sweet hot pineapple. Let each bite take you to warmer climes, wherever you might really be.

Jerk seasoning is a blended mix of ground hot peppers, dried thyme, allspice, cinnamon and cayenne pepper. You'll find it available in most supermarkets.

Heat the sunflower oil in a large frying pan over a medium–high heat and add the pineapple, red pepper and onion. Stir-fry for 4–5 minutes until softened and sticky.

Sprinkle in the jerk seasoning and cook for a further 3–4 minutes until bubbling and sticky.

Remove from the heat and season with smoked sea salt. Squeeze over the lime juice and sprinkle with the coriander.

Load into the tortillas and scatter with the sliced chilli and reserved onion rounds.

1 tbsp sunflower oil

½ small ripe pineapple, peeled and roughly sliced

1 red (bell) pepper, roughly sliced

1 small red onion, finely sliced into rounds, reserving a few raw rounds to garnish

1 rounded tsp jerk seasoning

Pinch of smoked sea salt

Juice of ½ unwaxed lime

Generous handful of fresh coriander (cilantro), roughly chopped

1–2 soft tortillas, warmed

1 small red chilli, deseeded and finely sliced

drunken beans

Serves 1

Serve these feisty, boozy beans with Jerk pulled pineapple (opposite).

Heat the sunflower oil in a small saucepan over a medium heat and cook the onion for 2 minutes until softened. Add the green chilli and garlic, and cook for a further minute.

Spoon in the chilli powder and kidney beans, and stir through.

Pour in the beer, then loosely cover with a lid and cook for 10 minutes, stirring frequently.

When the liquid has reduced, remove the pan from the heat. Stir through the coriander and serve hot.

1 tbsp sunflower oil

1 small red onion, finely chopped

1 green chilli, deseeded and roughly sliced

1 clove of garlic, crushed

½ tsp chilli powder

130g (4½oz) can red kidney beans, drained and rinsed

200ml (7fl oz/generous ¾ cup) beer (ensure vegan)

Small handful of fresh coriander (cilantro), finely chopped

moroccan flatbread pizza

Serves 1

Go home, kick off your shoes and make this pizza. It's everything a pizza should be – and then some.

———

Harissa is a spicy paste mix, made from chillies, tomatoes and rose water. You will find it in most supermarkets, or Middle Eastern shops and delis.

Heat the olive oil in a frying pan over a medium–high heat and cook the onion for 8 minutes until golden and softened.

Preheat the oven to 200°C/400°F/gas mark 6.

Mix together the tomato purée and harissa. Arrange the flatbread on a baking tray, then spread over the spicy tomato mixture.

Scatter over the spinach leaves, then drizzle with extra virgin olive oil. Spoon over the golden onion and scatter with the pine nuts.

Bake for 5–6 minutes until hot, then scatter with the pomegranate seeds and parsley. Squeeze over a little lemon juice just before serving.

1 tbsp olive oil

1 large onion, finely sliced

1 tbsp tomato purée

2 tsp harissa

1 large flatbread

Generous handful of baby spinach leaves

Generous drizzle of extra virgin olive oil

1 rounded tbsp pine nuts

1 tbsp pomegranate seeds

Small handful of fresh flat-leaf parsley, roughly torn

Juice of ¼ unwaxed lemon

black pepper courgette fries

Serves 1

Courgettes will become your new best friend after you've tried this simple recipe. The fries are brilliant served with Moroccan flatbread pizza (page 102).

Mix the flour with 50ml (1¾fl oz/scant ¼ cup) of cold water until you form a batter the consistency of double cream. Stir through the black pepper.

Heat the sunflower oil in a heavy-bottomed saucepan to 180°C (350°F), or until a small piece of courgette browns and rises to the surface when dropped in.

Dip the courgette chips into the batter, then carefully place in the oil, being careful not to overfill the pan. Fry for 3–4 minutes until golden and crisp.

Use a slotted spoon to remove the chips from the pan and drain on kitchen paper. Season with sea salt and extra black pepper to taste.

1 rounded tbsp plain (all-purpose) flour

1 tsp freshly ground black pepper, for the batter, plus extra to season

300ml (½ pint/1¼ cups) sunflower oil, for frying

1 medium courgette (zucchini), sliced into chips

Generous pinch of flaked sea salt, crushed

sides & bites

Treat yourself to something on the side with these seasonal dishes. This is the perfect collection of dips, sauces and snacks – comforting, tasty and fast.

spiced dukkah

Makes 1 small jar

Dukkah is a typically Egyptian condiment of toasted nuts and spices, usually served with breads and oils. It can also be sprinkled over salads to add texture and spice. I love it sprinkled over Green pea houmous (opposite), for a nutty and earthy crunch.

Store in a sealed jar for up to two weeks.

Preheat the oven to 200°C/400°F/gas mark 6.

Spread all the ingredients evenly onto a baking tray and bake for 8–10 minutes until toasted and golden.

Blitz in a high-powered blender until roughly chopped, but not dusty.

70g (2½oz/½ cup) blanched hazelnuts

3 tbsp sesame seeds

1 tbsp cumin seeds

1 tbsp fennel seeds

1 tbsp coriander seeds

1 tsp flaked sea salt

sides & bites

green pea houmous

Serves 2

Tender and fresh peas add a new taste to houmous. Serve with crudités or toasted pitta bread.

————

Tahini, or sesame seed paste, can be found in the supermarket world food aisle or in Middle Eastern shops.

Simmer the peas in boiling water for 2 minutes until heated through, then drain thoroughly.

Add the peas, lime juice, cumin, coriander and tahini to a high-powered blender and blitz until smooth.

Spoon out into a bowl and stir through the extra virgin olive oil. Season to taste with sea salt.

200g (7oz/1⅓ cups) frozen or fresh peas

Juice of 1 unwaxed lime

½ tsp ground cumin

Generous handful of fresh coriander (cilantro)

2 tbsp tahini

Generous glug of extra virgin olive oil

Generous pinch of sea salt

stir-fried chestnuts, cavolo nero and cranberries

Serves 2

These wintry and warming chestnuts make the perfect main dish when served with rice, or the perfect side dish for four people to go with a roast dinner.

You'll find cooked vacuum-packed chestnuts in most supermarkets. They have a long shelf life and are handy to keep in the cupboard for stir-fries, stuffing and rich puddings.

Heat the sunflower oil in a wok over a high heat until very hot, then sprinkle in the chilli flakes.

Add the chestnuts, cavolo nero and cranberries, and stir-fry for 3–4 minutes until the leaves become softened.

Remove from the heat and stir through the freshly squeezed orange juice and soy sauce until all the ingredients are coated.

1 tbsp sunflower oil

1 tsp dried chilli flakes

180g (6oz/1¼ cups) cooked vacuum-packed chestnuts, roughly sliced

6 large leaves of cavolo nero, roughly shredded and stems discarded

1 tbsp dried cranberries

Juice of ½ unwaxed orange

1 tsp dark soy sauce

grilled asparagus with soy and sesame

Serves 2

You know it's spring when vibrant British asparagus appears on your plate. I love asparagus when it's gently griddled and charred, however, it can be tricky to turn so many spears at once. This recipe groups a few spears together, so they can be turned easily and quickly.

This recipe also works well on the barbecue.

Heat a griddle pan over a medium–high heat while you prepare the asparagus.

Use a pre-soaked wooden (or metal) skewer to thread through the bottom end of the asparagus spears, then another to thread closer to the tip. Place four asparagus spears on this 'raft', then repeat for the remaining asparagus.

Use a pastry brush to coat the asparagus in the soy sauce, then place on the hot griddle pan for 3–4 minutes. Use tongs to turn the spears over when grill marks appear. Cook for 2–3 minutes on the other side.

Remove from the pan and carefully slide off the skewers. Scatter with the sesame seeds.

8 spears of asparagus, tough ends removed

1 tbsp dark soy sauce

2 tsp sesame seeds

sweetcorn fritters

Serves 2

I love this recipe for sweetcorn fritters, using ingredients from the store cupboard. These fritters are great for when your fridge is empty – and little fingers love them too! Try them dipped in sweet chilli sauce.

————

Baking powder gives rise to these fluffy fritters.

In a bowl, mix together the flour, baking powder, parsley and sea salt. Stir through 120ml (4¼fl oz/ ½ cup) cold water and whisk until smooth to make a batter.

Stir in the sweetcorn until coated in the batter.

Heat the sunflower oil in a frying pan over a medium heat. Place tablespoon-size dollops of batter into the hot oil and cook for 2–3 minutes on both sides until golden and slightly risen.

100g (3½oz/¾ cup) plain (all-purpose) flour

2 tsp baking powder

1 tsp dried parsley

½ tsp fine sea salt

200g (7oz/11/8 cups) sweetcorn, canned and drained, or frozen and defrosted before use

4 tbsp sunflower oil

broad bean bruschetta

Serves 4

Everyone loves bruschetta, with its hot and crispy base and fresh toppings. This seasonal twist will use up summer's broad beans in a delicious and very simple way.

Heat a griddle pan over a medium–high heat while you rub the garlic-infused olive oil onto one side of the baguette slices.

Place the slices oil-side down onto the pan and toast for 4–5 minutes until toasted with grill marks, then arrange on a plate.

Add the broad beans to a saucepan of simmering water and boil for 2–3 minutes until softened and vibrant. Drain and rinse the broad beans in cold water.

Add the beans to a bowl and semi-crush using a masher, crushing some beans and leaving others whole. Spoon in the vegan cream cheese and extra virgin olive oil, then stir in the parsley and chives.

Spoon the broad bean mixture over the toasted bread, pressing it down slightly to keep it in place.

Drizzle of garlic-infused olive oil

1 white baguette, thinly sliced into rounds

300g (10oz/1¾ cups) fresh broad (fava) beans, podded

3 rounded tbsp vegan cream cheese

Generous drizzle of extra virgin olive oil

Handful of fresh flat-leaf parsley, roughly chopped

Handful of chives, finely chopped

grilled peach, basil and walnut salad

Serves 2

There's something beautiful about hot, caramelised peaches placed over fragrant basil that makes this more than just a salad. Team with hot, toasted walnuts for added bite.

———

The slight bitterness of rapeseed oil works perfectly drizzled over this salad.

Heat a griddle pan over a high heat. Place the peaches cut-side down and cook for 4–5 minutes until caramelised with grill marks.

In the meantime, arrange the watercress, lamb's lettuce and basil over plates.

Place the hot peaches over the leaves while you carefully toast the walnuts in the pan for 30 seconds, then sprinkle them over the salad.

Drizzle with the rapeseed oil, season with black pepper and serve.

4 ripe peaches, halved and stones removed

2 generous handfuls of watercress

2 handfuls of lamb's lettuce

30g (1oz) fresh basil leaves

2 tbsp walnut pieces

Drizzle of extra virgin rapeseed oil

Pinch of black pepper

sides & bites

blackberry salsa

Makes 1 small jar

This dark and interesting salsa pairs well with Caramelised onion, thyme and fig tartlets (page 16), for a taste of autumn.

Fresh blackberries offer the most complex flavours, but frozen blackberries also work well; simply defrost fully before using.

In a mixing bowl, roughly mash the blackberries to release the juices.

Stir in the chilli, coriander, lime zest and juice, and maple syrup.

Season to taste with sea salt. This salsa will keep for 3–4 days in an airtight container in the fridge.

150g (5½oz/1¼ cups) blackberries

1 small green chilli, deseeded and finely chopped

Small handful of fresh coriander (cilantro), finely chopped

Zest and juice of 1 unwaxed lime

1 tsp maple syrup

Pinch of sea salt

sundried tomato pesto

Makes 1 small jar

Try this rich and flavourful pesto stirred through pasta or on bruschetta for added flavour. It's a vibrant twist on classic green pesto.

—————

No need to drain the oil from the sundried tomatoes before using, the extra oil helps to create a smooth pesto.

Pulse together the pine nuts, garlic and sea salt in a blender until crushed.

Add the sundried tomatoes, parsley and extra virgin olive oil, and blend until almost smooth.

This pesto will keep for up to 3 days in an airtight container in the fridge.

2 tbsp pine nuts

1 clove of garlic, peeled

Generous pinch of sea salt

250g (9oz/2½ cups) soft sundried tomatoes in oil

Generous handful of fresh flat-leaf parsley, torn

150ml (5¼fl oz/generous ½ cup) good-quality extra virgin olive oil

parsnip crisps

Serves 2

These crisp, sweet and salty crisps make a delicious snack or attractive addition to a main meal.

———

A sharp mandolin will thinly slice the parsnips enough to crisp in the hot oil, or use a fine slicer attachment on a food processor. If you possess patience, use a vegetable peeler to create the fine slices.

Heat the sunflower oil in a heavy-bottomed saucepan over a medium–high heat. Test if the temperature of the oil is hot enough by dropping one slice of parsnip into the pan – if it sizzles and rises to the top, the oil is ready.

In small batches, drop the parsnip slices into the pan and fry for 2–3 minutes until golden. Carefully remove and drain on kitchen paper while you cook the rest.

Season to taste with sea salt and allow to crisp up fully for a few minutes before serving.

300ml (½ pint/1¼ cups) sunflower oil

2 large parsnips, very finely sliced

Generous pinch of sea salt

sides & bites

warm blood orange salad

Serves 2

Simple, fresh and warming.

Heat a griddle pan over a high heat. Carefully place the orange slices onto the pan and cook for 2 minutes on each side.

In the meantime, combine the red onion, mint and rocket, and arrange on a serving plate.

Remove the orange slices from the pan and place over the leaves.

Throw the pistachios onto the hot pan and toast for a few seconds before spooning on top of the oranges.

Drizzle over the extra virgin olive oil and season to taste with sea salt.

2 unwaxed blood oranges, peeled and sliced into rounds

1 small red onion, finely sliced

Handful of fresh mint leaves, finely chopped

2 generous handfuls of wild rocket (arugula)

2 tbsp pistachios, shelled

Generous drizzle of extra virgin olive oil

Pinch of sea salt

skin-on seaside chips

Serves 2

I couldn't write this book without including my favourite comfort food: chips. Let this recipe transport you to the great British seaside, tucking into a bag of hot, vinegary chips by the sea.

Leaving the skin on the potatoes adds extra flavour, as well as being quicker to prepare. Simply scrub thoroughly before use.

Heat the sunflower oil in a deep-fat fryer to 130°C (265°F). If you don't have a deep-fat fryer, use a heavy-bottomed saucepan to heat the oil over a medium heat until a test chip sizzles and floats to the top.

Use a slotted spoon to carefully add the potato chips to the oil. Fry for 8 minutes until starting to golden, then remove and set aside.

Increase the heat of the deep-fat fryer 190°C (375°F), or if you're using a heavy-bottomed saucepan, increase the heat to high.

Carefully place the par-cooked chips back into the pan for a further 4–5 minutes until golden brown.

Serve while hot with malt vinegar and sea salt.

500ml (17½fl oz/2 cups) sunflower oil, for frying

2 large Maris Piper potatoes, chopped into chunky chips

Generous sprinkle of malt vinegar

Pinch of flaked sea salt

speedy
samosas

Serves 2

This recipe was born when I had a craving for samosas, but not enough time to make the traditional recipe. These speedy samosas have all of the authentic flavours you're familiar with, but use soft tortillas as the wrapping. Samosas in under 15 minutes? You'll be hooked.

Garam masala is a pre-mixed Indian spice blend, so keep a jar in the cupboard to save you time blending spices.

Preheat the oven to 200°C/400°F/gas mark 6.

Heat 1 tablespoon of sunflower oil in a frying pan over a medium–high heat and soften the onion for 1–2 minutes. Throw in the green beans, peas and carrot, and cook for a further 3 minutes, stirring frequently until the vegetables have started to soften. Sprinkle in the garam masala, stir through to coat the vegetables and cook for a further minute. Squeeze in the lemon juice and stir.

Cut the tortillas in half. Place one-quarter of the filling onto each tortilla half, then fold to create a triangle. Use a pastry brush to apply a little sunflower oil along the inside edges of the samosas to seal them. Then brush a little over the top of the samosas. Bake for 5–6 minutes until golden. Serve hot or cold.

1 tbsp sunflower oil, plus 2 tsp for brushing and sealing

1 small red onion, finely chopped

8 green beans, finely chopped

1 tbsp frozen peas

1 carrot, grated

2 tsp garam masala

Juice of 1 unwaxed lemon

2 soft tortillas

sides & bites

sweet

Rich, sweet treats and puddings from childhood
make for some of the best comfort foods,
whatever your age.

instant mango fro-yo

Serves 2 generously

When I lived in the city, I loved eating a tub of frozen yoghurt on a hot day. I was lucky to find a wonderful shop (that I passed on my way home from work throughout summer) that sold a vegan version. No matter where you are, stopping and having a moment of calm is good for the mind and body; this instant fro-yo will transport you to somewhere tropical.

—

Frozen mango chunks are available in large supermarkets. Stock up and use them in smoothies, puddings and curries.

Add the frozen mango, coconut yoghurt and lime juice to a high-powered blender and blitz until smooth and creamy. Serve immediately.

200g (7oz/½ cup) frozen mango chunks

5 rounded tbsp coconut yoghurt

Juice of 1 unwaxed lime

lemon curd

Makes 1 medium jar

Creamy, zesty lemon curd, generously spread onto white bread, brings back memories of childhood summers spent in the garden. I always have a small jar of this in the fridge – I hope you will too.

Traditionally, lemon curd is made using eggs and butter. This vegan version sets as it cools, however, I love it straight from the pan, drizzled onto hot toast or over a vanilla cake. If you prefer a more set version, pour into a clean jar and leave overnight in the fridge.

Add the lemon zest, lemon juice, sugar, soya milk and cornflour to a pan, and bring to the boil over a medium–high heat. Simmer for 10 minutes, stirring frequently.

Stir through the vegan butter and cook for a further 2 minutes until smooth and glossy.

Use as a thickened drizzle while warm, or allow to cool and pour into a jar to set overnight. It will keep in the fridge for up to a week.

Zest and juice of 2 unwaxed lemons

150g (5½oz/¾ cup) granulated sugar

400ml (14fl oz/scant 1¾ cups) sweetened soya milk

1 level tbsp cornflour (cornstarch)

1 tbsp vegan butter

rhubarb and cardamom fool

Serves 4

Being a Yorkshire girl, I love early season pink rhubarb, mainly grown in the beautiful county. This recipe combines the gently smoked flavour of cardamom with a tangy rhubarb purée, layered with smooth vanilla yoghurt. This dessert tastes wonderful when the yoghurt is ice cold and the rhubarb hot, but is equally delicious when served chilled, meaning it can be made and assembled in advance.

—————

Cardamom seeds are best freshly crushed from pods, using a pestle and mortar. Ground cardamom from the jar is convenient, but lacks the same fresh-flavour burst.

Preheat the oven to 200°C/400°F/gas mark 6.

Arrange the rhubarb evenly onto a baking tray and scatter with the sugar and ground cardamom. Spoon over 1 tablespoon of cold water and cover with foil. Bake for 12 minutes until softened.

Remove the tray from the oven and carefully spoon the hot ingredients (including any juices) into a high-powered blender. Blitz until semi-smooth.

Add a spoonful of the rhubarb purée to small serving glasses, followed by a spoonful of yoghurt. Layer until complete.

Top with a mint leaf before serving.

6 sticks of forced rhubarb (about 500g/1lb 2oz), cut into even 2cm (¾in) pieces

3 tbsp caster (superfine) sugar

4 cardamom pods, crushed and seeds ground, shells discarded

12 tbsp vanilla soya yoghurt

4 mint leaves

marmalade and nutmeg rice pudding

Serves 2 generously

This is my favourite rainy-day food. When it's grey and drizzly outside, soothe yourself with a brightening bowl of sweetly spiced rice pudding with marmalade.

———

Flaked pudding rice has a shorter cooking time than standard pudding rice, so it can be made into a rich, creamy dessert in no time.

Add the pudding rice, almond milk and sugar to a pan and simmer over a medium–high heat for 5 minutes.

Stir through the nutmeg and cinnamon, and cook for a further 5 minutes, stirring frequently.

Serve in bowls before spooning over a generous scoop of the marmalade on each.

100g (3½oz/½ cup) flaked pudding rice

800ml (scant 1½ pints/ 3½ cups) sweetened almond milk

3 rounded tbsp caster (superfine) sugar

½ tsp freshly grated nutmeg

Pinch of ground cinnamon

2 tbsp thick-cut orange marmalade

pink lemonade

Makes about 1 litre (1¾ pints/4½ cups)

This homemade lemonade makes me think of picnics with wicker baskets, gingham cloths and cucumber sandwiches. Whether you're going on a picnic or simply in need of a sweet drink, this pink lemonade is refreshing, zingy and beautifully cloudy.

Shop-bought pink lemonade may be coloured with carmine, which is a pink-red pigment obtained from a species of insect. Carmine can also be listed as cochineal or E120, and this additive isn't suitable for vegans.

Add the lemon zest and juice, sugar and raspberries to a saucepan and bring to a simmer over a medium heat for 5 minutes until the sugar has dissolved.

Remove from the heat and pour in the icy water.

Sieve the lemonade into a jug and discard the cooked ingredients.

Pour the lemonade into ice-filled glasses.

Zest and juice of 6 unwaxed lemons

200g (7oz/1 cup) caster (superfine) sugar

100g (3½oz/¾ cup) raspberries

1 litre (1¾ pints/4½ cups) icy water

Ice cubes, for serving

apple mojito

Serves 1

I fondly remember the first mojito I ever tried. It was so refreshing, icy and fragrant, and remains my favourite cocktail. This twist on the classic is sweet and long, perfect for an afternoon spent in the garden with friends.

In a tall glass, gently muddle the mint leaves and lime juice to release the flavours.

Scoop in the ice and pour over the white rum.

Top up with the apple juice and serve with wedges of lime.

10 fresh mint leaves

Juice of ½ unwaxed lime, other ½ cut into wedges and reserved for serving

Generous scoop of crushed ice

50ml (1¾fl oz/scant ¼ cup) white rum

200ml (7fl oz/generous ¾ cup) good-quality carbonated apple juice

chocolate
pretzel freakshake

Serves 1

Why choose between something sweet or salted when you can have both? Just get freakshaking!

Many flavours and brands of vegan ice cream are available in large supermarkets and health food shops. Try them all and decide on your favourite!

Heat the chocolate for 2–3 minutes in a heatproof bowl over a pan of simmering water until melted.

In the meantime, whisk together the chocolate soya milk and peanut butter in a wide-necked jug until combined, then pour into a tall glass or jar.

Spoon over the chocolate and vanilla ice creams.

Use a spoon to drizzle over some of the melted chocolate onto the ice cream.

Press on the pretzels and popcorn, and drizzle with the remaining melted chocolate.

4 squares of dark chocolate (ensure dairy free)

200ml (7fl oz/generous ¾ cup) chilled chocolate soya milk

2 tsp smooth peanut butter

1 scoop of vegan chocolate ice cream

1 scoop of vegan vanilla ice cream

6 small salted pretzels

Small handful of salted popcorn

cherry
pot pies

Makes 4

Dark, juicy cherries are sweet, sticky and zesty in these golden pastry-topped pies. Pitted cherries are a useful ingredient to keep in the freezer for fruity pies or for whipping into smoothies when the fruit is out of season. These pies are topped with puff pastry for a rustic taste of home.

———

Many brands of shop-bought puff pastry use vegetable oils instead of butter, making it accidentally vegan. Always check the ingredients.

Preheat the oven to 200°C/400°F/gas mark 6.

Place four ramekin pots over the pastry and cut around them with a knife. Place the rounds of pastry onto a non-stick baking tray and brush the tops with a little soya milk. Bake for 10–12 minutes until golden and nicely puffed.

In the meantime, add the cherries, lemon juice and caster sugar to a pan and bring to a bubble over a medium heat, stirring frequently for 10 minutes until the sugar has dissolved and created a dark sauce.

Spoon the cherries and sticky sauce into the ramekins.

Remove the pastry lids from the oven and carefully place them on top of the cherry filling. Sprinkle over a little icing sugar. Serve hot.

1 sheet of pre-rolled puff pastry (ensure dairy-free)

1 tsp soya milk, for glazing

300g (10oz/1¾ cups) frozen or fresh pitted cherries

Juice of 1 unwaxed lemon

2 tbsp caster (superfine) sugar

Sprinkle of icing (confectioners') sugar

sweet

ginger snap cookies

Makes about 8

Crisp along the edges and chewy in the centre, these ginger snap cookies are the perfect bake. Even the sweet aroma reminds me of home! When you remove these cookies from the oven, they will be soft, but after a few minutes of cooling they will be a perfect crisp texture.

———

Depending on the brand of vegan butter you use (as they vary in oil content) you may need to add a little extra flour before rolling the dough into balls if it appears too sticky.

Preheat the oven to 180°C/350°F/gas mark 4 and line a baking tray with greaseproof paper.

Heat the sugar, vegan butter and golden syrup in a saucepan over a low–medium heat for 3–4 minutes until combined into a glossy sauce.

Stir together the flour, ginger and cinnamon in a mixing bowl.

Pour the hot syrup into the flour mix and stir until a dough is formed.

Roll teaspoon-sized small balls of dough in your hands and press onto the prepared baking tray. They will spread a little, so leave some space between each cookie. Use the tines of a fork to press over and flatten each ball. Bake for 10 minutes, then carefully remove and place on a wire rack to cool.

50g (1¾oz/¼ cup) caster (superfine) sugar

50g (1¾oz/3½ tbsp) vegan butter

2 tbsp golden syrup

150g (5½oz/1 cup plus 2 tbsp) self-raising flour

2 tsp ground ginger

½ tsp ground cinnamon

cookie dough for one

Serves 1

It's no secret of mine that many batches of dough intended to be cookies never make it into the oven. I love cookie dough so much that I've created this treat for one. It combines soft brown sugar for that authentic, grainy texture, but if you prefer your dough smooth, switch the sugar for maple syrup.

———

For a fast dessert, stir the cookie dough through vegan vanilla ice cream.

In a small bowl, fork together the vegan butter and sugar.

Stir through the flour and vanilla extract until combined.

Sprinkle through the chocolate chips.

2 tbsp vegan butter, softened

2 tbsp soft brown sugar

3 rounded tbsp plain (all-purpose) flour

1 tsp vanilla extract

1 tbsp dark chocolate chips (ensure dairy free)

turkish delight melt-in-the-middle mug cake

Serves 1

When the need for indulgent chocolate cake arises, this 2-minute mug cake satisfies on every level. You'll spoon through soft, warm cake before you reach a sweet, gooey centre. You're welcome.

In a large mug, mix together the flour, cocoa powder and sugar until combined.

Pour in the sunflower oil, 3 tablespoons of cold water and the rose extract, then whisk with a fork until combined and smooth.

Press the Turkish delight into the centre of the mug until it is completely covered in batter.

Cook in a 800W microwave for 2 minutes and allow to cool for 1 minute before digging in.

2 tbsp self-raising flour

2 tbsp cocoa powder

2 tbsp caster (superfine) sugar

1 tbsp sunflower oil

¼ tsp rose extract

2 squares of Turkish delight (ensure gelatine free and carmine free), more to garnish

vanilla poached victoria plums

Serves 4

Sweetly sticky, hot and juicy Victoria plums are always a good idea.

This recipe is a great way to use unripened plums.

Add the halved plums to a large saucepan and spoon over the caster sugar.

Halve the vanilla pod lengthways, then scrape the seeds into the pan. Spoon in the nutmeg and add the cinnamon stick.

Pour over the hot water and turn the heat to a medium–high. Cook for 10–12 minutes until the sugar has dissolved and the plums have softened. Remove the cinnamon stick and serve hot.

10 Victoria plums, halved and stones removed

200g (7oz/1 cup) caster (superfine) sugar

1 vanilla pod (bean)

1 tsp freshly grated nutmeg

1 cinnamon stick

300ml (½ pint/1¼ cups) hot water

biscuit-baked clementines with amaretto

Serves 4

These juicy, boozy baked clementines are topped with crunchy biscuits and almonds. Serve with a scoop of vegan ice cream for a comforting pudding.

———

'Accidentally' vegan-friendly caramel biscuits can be found in many supermarkets; do check the ingredients as brands change their recipes from time to time.

Preheat the oven to 200°C/400°F/gas mark 6.

Cut 6 of the clementines in half widthways and then arrange cut-side up in a deep baking tray.

Squeeze the juice from the remaining clementine into a bowl, then whisk in the liqueur and maple syrup.

Pour the juice-syrup over and around the clementines, then loosely cover with foil. Bake for 10 minutes.

Remove the baking tray from the oven and sprinkle the crushed biscuits and flaked almonds over the clementines. Return to the oven, without the foil, for 2–3 minutes. Serve hot.

7 clementines, peeled

1 tbsp amaretto liqueur

1 tbsp maple syrup

4 caramel biscuits (ensure vegan), roughly crushed

1 tsp flaked (slivered) almonds

coffee and cream french toast

Serves 4

Serve this indulgent delight for breakfast, brunch or dessert (or any time in between).

Heat the sunflower oil in a griddle pan over a medium heat while you prepare the batter.

Add the coffee granules and boiling water to a large bowl to dissolve the grains. Pour in the almond milk, syrup, vanilla extract and flour, and use a balloon whisk to mix the batter until smooth.

Dip a slice of bread into the batter and coat on both sides, then use tongs to place on the hot griddle pan. Turn after 2 minutes and cook until golden and crisp. Repeat with each slice of bread, keeping the other slices warm on top of each other on a plate lined with kitchen paper to soak up excess oil. When all the bread has been grilled, arrange on plates.

Mix together the sugar, cinnamon and cocoa powder, and sprinkle over the toasts. Add a scoop of vanilla ice cream and serve.

4 tbsp sunflower oil

1 rounded tsp strong instant coffee granules

2 tsp boiling water

200ml (7fl oz/generous ¾ cup) sweetened almond milk

2 tbsp maple syrup

1 tsp vanilla extract

100g (3½oz/¾ cup) plain (all-purpose) flour

4 slices of thick white bread

4 tsp caster (superfine) sugar

½ tsp ground cinnamon

½ tsp cocoa powder

4 scoops of vegan vanilla ice cream

jam
sponge
pudding

Serves 2

Readers of my first cookbook, *15 Minute Vegan*, will know that one of my favourite desserts from childhood is syrup sponge pudding. I also love this version cooked with jam, which always has to be strawberry.

The purpose of adding the cider vinegar to the soya milk is to create a vegan buttermilk for a silky sponge pudding.

In a bowl, whisk together the soya milk and cider vinegar, and set aside to curdle.

In a large mixing bowl, cream together the sugar and vegan butter until pale in colour. Mix in the flour and baking powder, and fold until combined.

Pour in the curdled soya milk and stir through until incorporated.

Spoon the strawberry jam into a medium microwave-safe bowl, then gently pour over the cake batter. Cook in a 800W microwave for 3 minutes until the sponge appears set.

Allow to stand for 1 minute before carefully turning out onto a plate. Serve hot.

100ml (3½fl oz/scant ½ cup) soya milk

1 tsp apple cider vinegar

50g (1¾oz/¼ cup) caster (superfine) sugar

50g (1¾oz/3½ tbsp) vegan butter

100g (3½oz/¾ cup) self-raising flour

½ tsp baking powder

3 rounded tbsp strawberry jam

sweet

honeycomb

Makes 1 small batch

These golden shards of caramelised sugar remind me of autumn months, keeping warm by the bonfire and sharing sweet treats with friends.

Add the sugar and golden syrup to a large saucepan. Cook over a high heat for 3–4 minutes without stirring until the mixture starts to bubble and becomes the colour of maple syrup.

Remove from the heat and use a balloon whisk to vigorously whisk in the bicarbonate of soda.

Pour the mixture into a shallow non-stick baking tray and leave to cool for 10 minutes until the top appears shiny and crisp. Break into uneven pieces and store in a sealed container for up to 2 days.

100g (3½oz/½ cup) granulated sugar

4 tbsp golden syrup

1½ tsp bicarbonate of soda (baking soda)

peanut butter cheesecake shots

Serves 4

Smooth peanut butter makes for the most silken, smooth filling in these cheesecake shots. Best served in small glasses or shot glasses, because they are so rich.

————

Many supermarket own-brand digestive biscuits don't contain cow's milk, but always check the ingredients.

Soften the peanut butter in a bowl, then pour in the soya cream and use a fork or balloon whisk to beat to a thick, creamy consistency.

In a small saucepan, melt the vegan butter over a low heat while you break the biscuits into a breadcrumb consistency, either using a food processor, blender or by adding them to a food bag and beating with a rolling pin. Remove the pan from the heat, then pour the biscuit crumbs into the pan and stir to combine.

Allow the biscuit mixture to cool for a few minutes, then press into the bottom of small glasses. Spoon in the peanut butter mixture and finish with a sprinkle of chocolate chips. The cheesecake shots can be refrigerated for 2 hours before serving for a gently chilled dessert.

3 tbsp smooth peanut butter, at room temperature

100ml (3½fl oz/scant ½ cup) soya single (light) cream

1 rounded tbsp vegan butter

6 digestive biscuits (graham crackers), ensure dairy free

4 tsp dark chocolate chips (ensure dairy free)

sweet

banana fritters

Serves 2

I spent some of my childhood in Hong Kong and although I don't remember much more than bright lights and busy markets, I do remember eating sweet banana fritters. A light, crisp batter encases the hot and caramelised banana – once tasted, never forgotten.

Combine the flour, sesame seeds and cinnamon in a mixing bowl, then pour in the sparkling water and use a balloon whisk to form a smooth batter.

Heat the sunflower oil in a heavy-bottomed pan over a medium heat, then drop in a small amount of the batter to test if the oil is hot enough – if a teaspoon of the batter sizzles and becomes golden within 30 seconds, the oil is at optimum temperature.

Dip the banana slices into the batter, then carefully place a few pieces in the hot oil for 2–3 minutes until golden. Remove from the oil using a slotted spoon and drain on kitchen paper until all the banana pieces are cooked.

Serve hot with Miso caramel sauce (opposite) or a scoop of vegan vanilla ice cream.

100g (3½oz/¾ cup) self-raising flour

1 tsp sesame seeds

½ tsp ground cinnamon

200ml (7fl oz/generous ¾ cup) sparkling water

400ml (14fl oz/scant 1¾ cups) sunflower oil, for frying

2 bananas, peeled and chopped in half widthways, then lengthways (into 8 pieces in total)

sweet

miso caramel sauce

Makes 1 small jar

Meet salted caramel's sophisticated big sister. White miso adds a salty, umami depth to a sweet, smooth caramel sauce. Serve hot with banana fritters (opposite) or use as a dipping sauce when cooled.

Miso is a natural flavouring made from fermented soya beans. It adds depth to sweet and savoury dishes, and lasts well in the fridge.

Melt the sugar, golden syrup, vegan butter, vanilla extract and miso paste in a saucepan over a low heat for 5–6 minutes without stirring.

Remove from the heat and allow to cool for a few minutes, then whisk in the soya cream until silken and smooth.

3 tbsp soft brown sugar

2 rounded tbsp golden syrup

1 rounded tbsp vegan butter

1 tsp vanilla extract

1 tsp white miso paste

200ml (7fl oz/generous ¾ cup) soya single (light) cream

white chocolate fondue

Serves 2

Who doesn't love silky, melted chocolate?
Use bright berries and vegan marshmallows to dip into this luxurious sweet fondue.

———

Vegan white chocolate can be found in the free-from sections of most supermarkets, or in health food shops. Vegan white chocolate buttons work well in this recipe, too!

To make the fondue, add the white chocolate and soya cream to a heatproof bowl. Halve the vanilla pod lengthways, then scrape the seeds into the bowl.

Bring a small saucepan of water to a simmer, then set the bowl over the pan to create a bain-marie. Stir occasionally for 5–6 minutes until the chocolate has melted and combines with the cream.

Pour into a fondue bowl and keep warm with a tea light.

Serve with blackberries, cherries, strawberries and vegan marshmallows to dip.

For the fondue
200g (7oz) vegan white chocolate, broken into pieces

200ml (7fl oz/generous ¾ cup) soya single (light) cream

1 vanilla pod (bean)

To serve
6 blackberries

6 cherries

6 strawberries

6 vegan marshmallows (ensure gelatine and carmine free)

marshmallow fluff

Makes 1 jar

Do you ever longingly look at the jars of American-style marshmallow fluff and dream about spooning it over pancakes or loading it onto cupcakes? Well this recipe is the answer. It uses a product called 'aquafaba', which is the water from a can of chickpeas, and has long been used as an egg substitute. It's often used in vegan meringues, mousses, mayonnaise and this sweet marshmallow fluff.

Cream of tartar can be found in supermarket baking aisles.

Add the icing sugar and chickpea water to a stand mixer bowl and whisk on high for 5 minutes.

Add the cream of tartar and vanilla extract, and whisk for a further 10 minutes until whipped and creamy.

60g (2oz/½ cup) icing (confectioners') sugar

Unsalted water drained from 400g (14oz) can chickpeas (reserve the chickpeas for another recipe)

½ tsp cream of cream of tartar

1 tsp vanilla extract

sweet

coconut popcorn

Serves 2

Movie night wouldn't be the same without a bowl of popcorn to nibble on. This sweet recipe is addictive and cheaper than the pre-flavoured microwave versions.

Melt the coconut oil in a large saucepan over a medium heat.

Add 2 or 3 popcorn kernels to the oil and when they become puffed into popcorn, remove these test ones and add the coconut extract to the pan, followed by the remaining kernels.

Cover the pan with a lid and wait 30 seconds, listening for the 'pop' sound. Shake the pan a few times to ensure even popping.

Remove the pan from the heat, keeping the lid on for a minute or so until the popping stops altogether. Stir through the desiccated coconut. Serve warm.

3 tbsp coconut oil

70g (2½oz/½ cup, plus 1 tsp) popcorn kernels

1 tsp coconut extract or essence (flavouring)

1 tbsp desiccated (dry unsweetened) coconut

carrot cake flapjacks

Makes about 8 squares

When visiting my favourite vegan bakery, I find it difficult to choose between a slice of carrot cake and a square of chewy flapjack (it's not unheard of for me to buy both). When I'm not able to visit the bakery, I bake carrot cake flapjacks and remember why I love these treats so much.

———

Use golden syrup and sunflower oil to reduce the cooking time of these flapjacks, as you don't have to spend additional time melting vegan butter and dissolving granulated sugar.

Preheat the oven to 200°C/400°F/gas mark 6.

Line a 30 x 20cm (12 x 8in) baking tray that's 3cm (1¼in) deep with baking paper.

In a large mixing bowl, mix together the sunflower oil, golden syrup, cinnamon and nutmeg until combined.

Tip in the oats, raisins and walnuts, and stir vigorously to coat in the syrup mixture, then stir through the carrot.

Press the mixture into the prepared baking tray, using the back of a spoon to smooth the top. Bake for 12 minutes, then allow to cool in the tin before slicing into even squares. The flapjacks will become firmer and chewy when cool.

4 tbsp sunflower oil

4 rounded tbsp golden syrup

1 tsp ground cinnamon

½ tsp ground nutmeg

150g (5½oz/1¾ cups) rolled oats

1 tbsp raisins

1 tbsp chopped walnuts

1 carrot, roughly grated

sweet

chocolate ganache-dipped churros

Serves 2 generously

Spanish-style churros are the ultimate sweet finger-food, perfect for dipping into a thick, chocolate ganache. The quantity of the ganache is generous, so you can relax the double-dipping rules.

Start by making the churros. Add 250ml (8¾fl oz/1 cup) of cold water, 2 tablespoons of sunflower oil, the sugar and salt to a saucepan and bring to a simmer over a medium heat.

Tip in the flour and mix together until a firm ball of dough is formed.

Heat the sunflower oil for frying in a deep-fat fryer or in a heavy-bottomed pan until it reaches 180°C (350°F) and a small piece of the dough turns golden within 1 minute. While the oil is coming to temperature, push all the dough into a large piping bag fitted with a star-shaped nozzle.

Squeeze 8cm (3¼in) pieces of dough into the hot oil, using clean scissors to cut each from the nozzle.

Cook the churros in the oil for 2–3 minutes until golden. When golden, keep warm by placing together and drain the excess oil on kitchen paper.

For the dusting, mix together the sugar and cinnamon on a plate, then roll the cooked churros in to coat.

To make the ganache, add the chocolate to a heatproof bowl and place over a pan of simmering water, stirring for 3–4 minutes until melted.

Stir the melted chocolate into the coconut cream, then stir through until fully combined.

Serve the hot churros in a bowl, with a generous helping of chocolate ganache for dipping.

sweet

For the churros
2 tbsp sunflower oil

3 tbsp caster (superfine) sugar

½ tsp fine salt

125g (4½oz/1 cup) plain
(all-purpose) flour

800ml (scant 1½ pints/3½
cups) sunflower oil, for frying

For the dusting
2 tbsp caster (superfine) sugar

½ tsp ground cinnamon

For the chocolate ganache
200ml (7fl oz/generous ¾ cup)
dark chocolate, broken into
pieces (ensure dairy free)

150ml (5¼fl oz/generous
½ cup) carton of thick
coconut cream

index

acknowledgements

Once again, I find myself in the (very fortunate) position of not knowing where to start thanking everyone involved in creating this beautiful book.

Firstly, a big thank you to the incredible team at Quadrille Publishing. Heartfelt thank you to publishing director Sarah Lavelle for believing in this idea, and to commissioning editor Zena Alkayat for the smooth running of the project and attention to detail. Further thanks for the editorial support of Corinne Masciocchi, Kathy Steer and Hilary Bird. A huge thanks to senior publicist Rebecca Smedley – you did such an amazing job with the first book and I'm looking forward to working with you again (I'll bring flapjacks). Thank you to Helen Lewis, Nathan Grace, Emily Lapworth and the design team for the beautiful layout and look – it's everything I imagined.

Thank you to photographer Dan Jones and assistant Aloha Bonser-Shaw for the incredible photographs. It was a pleasure to work with you. To the wonderful and talented food stylist Emily Ezekiel and assistant Kitty Coles, a huge thank you for your skill, patience and humour throughout the shoot. Prepare for an endless supply of Battenberg next time.

My wonderful literary agent Victoria Hobbs at A.M. Heath – thank you for making all of my dreams come true and for being a wonderful person to know.

A loving thank you to my wonderful parents for your ongoing support and encouragement. Thank you for always having food at the centre of every celebration and for showing me the true meaning of comfort food. I'm sure you'll find versions of your own recipes in here! Thanks for everything you do, you're incredible people.

Thank you to my fabulous sister Carolyne and brother-in-law Mark for believing in me. I'm so proud of your achievements and love you very much. To my star baker nieces Tamzin and Tara, what beautiful, bright and funny girls you are growing up to be. I hope you enjoy this book in your cookbook collection. Thank you also to my ever supportive Auntie May.

My amazing best friends Mary-Anne, Louise, Charlotte, Amelia, Emma, Amy and Katie – what would I do without you? Thank you for your honesty, encouragement, coffee dates and for keeping my feet on the ground. I'm so proud of you all.

Dudley, you remain my favourite writing partner. Thank you for all the cuddles.

Until every cage is empty.

publishing director: Sarah Lavelle
creative director: Helen Lewis
editor: Zena Alkayat
designers: Nathan Grace and Emily Lapworth
photographer: Dan Jones
food and props stylist: Emily Ezekiel
production: Nikolaus Ginelli, Vincent Smith

First published in 2018 by Quadrille, an imprint of Hardie Grant

Quadrille
52–54 Southwark Street
London SE1 1UN
quadrille.com